D1797233

CINECITTÀ

Federico Fellini

CINECITTÀ

060824

translated by Graham Fawcett

STUDIO
VISTA

First published in Great Britain in 1989
by Studio Vista
an imprint of Cassell Publishers Limited
Artillery House, Artillery Row
London SW1P 1RT

Translated by Graham Fawcett

Picture research by Gianfranco Angelucci and Daniela Barbiani

The drawings, reproduced by kind permission of Diogenes Verlag and
Editori Laterza, are by Federico Fellini

Quoted matter in the captions is by Federico Fellini

British Library Cataloguing in Publication Data
Fellini, Federico
  Fellini's Cinecittà.
  1. Italian cinema films. Directing. Fellini,
  Federico – critical studies
  I. Title   II. Un regista a Cinecittà. *English*
  791.43'0233'0924

  ISBN 0-289-80028-5

Filmset by Rowland Phototypesetting Limited, Bury St Edmunds, Suffolk

Printed and bound in Italy by Arnoldo Mondadori Editore, Verona

CONTENTS

"I was in a room that had no windows. It felt uncanny, but at the same time familiar. I moved about slowly, in pitch darkness. My hands touched a wall and followed it, but the wall was never-ending. In other films of mine, in dreams like this, I would fly away to freedom. This time, however, perhaps because I was not so light any more, it was an enormous struggle getting off the ground. Finally I made it, and there I was hovering thousands of feet up in the air. Glimpsing through gaps in the clouds at the landscape beneath me, I thought I saw the university campus. It might have been the hospital. No, it looked more like a prison, or a nuclear fall-out shelter. Eventually I realized what it was. It was Cinecittà."

That was the little story I told at the beginning of my film *Intervista*. It was my way of responding to a team of television journalists from Japan who had come to Cinecittà to interview me about the most famous film production center in Europe. What a relief it would be if I could feel the same spontaneity for the introduction I have been asked to write for this book. But I fear that it will not work out like that, and I shall have to think hard about it even though I honestly believe I said it all in *Intervista*, a short film which some of you may have seen.

I cannot trust myself to put this in the right way, but Cinecittà seems to me to belong to a time gone by, and I really do not think that I am the person best suited to discuss it with the historical, technical and general perspective which perhaps is called for here. The way I see things is always so subjective, so personal and single-minded, that I can only tell you the story of Cinecittà as I have witnessed and lived it; in other words, the Cinecittà of my own experience, the one in my films. It is true that I have spent many years of my life there. I have effectively taken up residence and even spent many a Sunday afternoon within its walls: not because it felt like home but rather because I so appreciated the quiet, almost clinical atmosphere in which I could work in peace and on my own without people forever calling my name and endless telephones to answer.

I do not feel particularly attached to Cinecittà either and if, as sometimes happens, I drive past, I can be completely

Perchè l'Italia Fascista diffonda nel mondo più rapida la luce della civiltà di Roma

Roma - Stabilimenti Cinematografici

CINECITTÀ

On pages 2 and 6: Cinecittà recreated at Cinecittà, like everything in the world of reality of Federico Fellini, for the 1987 film Intervista *(Fellini's* Intervista*). The model enabled Fellini to conjure up his creative kingdom, the place where he has made all his films since 1960. "I could have taken a series of shots of Cinecittà from a helicopter, but the result would have been an aerial view of the place and therefore too real to be effective. No, I wanted to do Cinecittà in a different way: by using the model, I was able to re-route the avenues of pine-trees, give the tarmac roofs a different colour, and make the buildings all the same grey colour as though they had come out of a child's model village kit."*
Above: A poster exploiting Cinecittà as an instrument of

Fascist propaganda. Indeed Cinecittà started out as a Fascist version of Hollywood, part of a dream of emulation which Mussolini's son Vittorio in particular sought to implant in the minds of an impoverished, megalomaniac Italy. Cinecittà was built in 475 days by Carlo Roncoroni to a design by the architect Gino Peressutti, at a very fast pace and with excellent results. Fifty years later, the buildings and studios in the rationalist style have not changed very much from how they looked in the original photographs and the artist's impression on the opposite page. The motto in the top left-hand corner of the poster reads: "So that Fascist Italy may spread more quickly through the world the splendour of the civilization of Rome."

oblivious to it. Its presence only dawns on me later, by which time I am caught up in the stream of traffic along Rome's Tuscolana highway, heading either back into town or out into open country on my way to a favourite little trattoria. I do not even pause to reflect that inside that edifice with the reddish-coloured walls, often covered in grubby posters with graffiti protesting outrage or love, is something which has determined, and still determines, the outcome of a great many episodes in my life. I tend generally to shy away from anything that reveals me so unequivocally; but, then, I promised I would write something, so let me see if I can pull it all together.

As to where and when I first heard about Cinecittà, where else could it have been other than that dusty, dingy and dilapidated old picture-palace, the Fulgor in Rimini? I could trace the origins of my whole life back to that little cinema. Its auditorium, I remember, was long and narrow and in summertime the commissionaire we all called "Usciaza" had to prevent the packed audiences from suffocating by opening the side exits. If passers-by peered in through the doorways, he used to bawl at them like a lunatic, shove them backwards into the street and close the curtains again. "Usciaza" was a nickname in Romagna dialect suggesting, rather irreverently, an usher of very large proportions.

He was huge, and when the Fulgor cinema was closed, he used to work in the railway goods yard unloading trucks. He was also very furtive, positioning himself behind the curtains when the lights went down and spying on the audience to see if any face betrayed the slightest hint of disloyalty when Mussolini appeared on the screen during the newsreels. Furthermore, he would not hesitate to report anybody suspect to the local Fascist headquarters.

One time, four people in the audience rolled him up in the curtain, tied the roll above his head and below his ankles, and left him spinning like a salami strung up to the ceiling. He howled like a wild beast from inside, but nobody had the nerve to go and set him free.

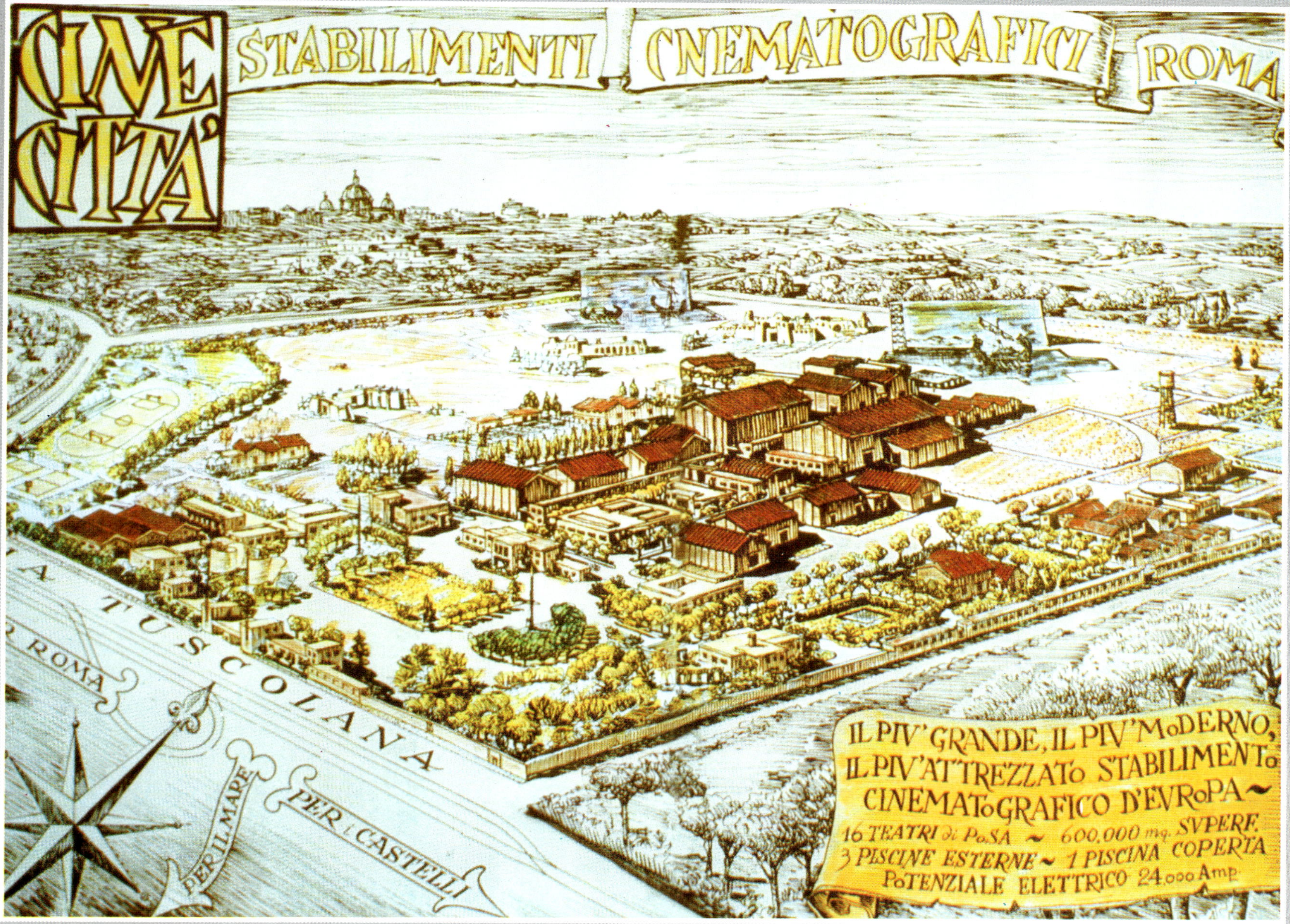
CINE CITTA'
STABILIMENTI
CNEMATOGRAFICI
ROMA
A TUSCOLANA
ROMA
PER IL MARE
PER i CASTELLI
IL PIV' GRANDE, IL PIV' MODERNO,
IL PIV' ATTREZZATO STABILIMENTO
CINEMATOGRAFICO D'EVROPA ~
16 TEATRI di POSA ~ 600.000 mq. SVPERF.
3 PISCINE ESTERNE ~ 1 PISCINA COPERTA
POTENZIALE ELETTRICO 24.000 Amp.

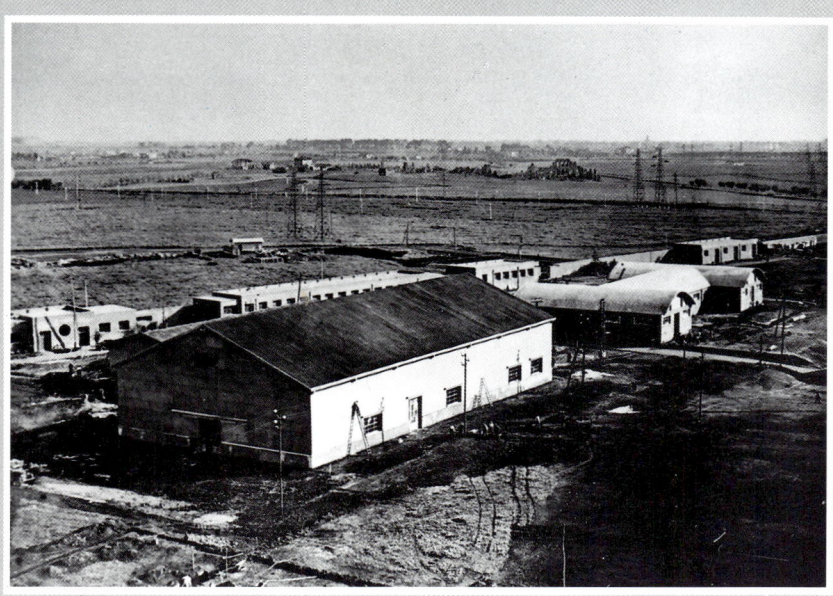

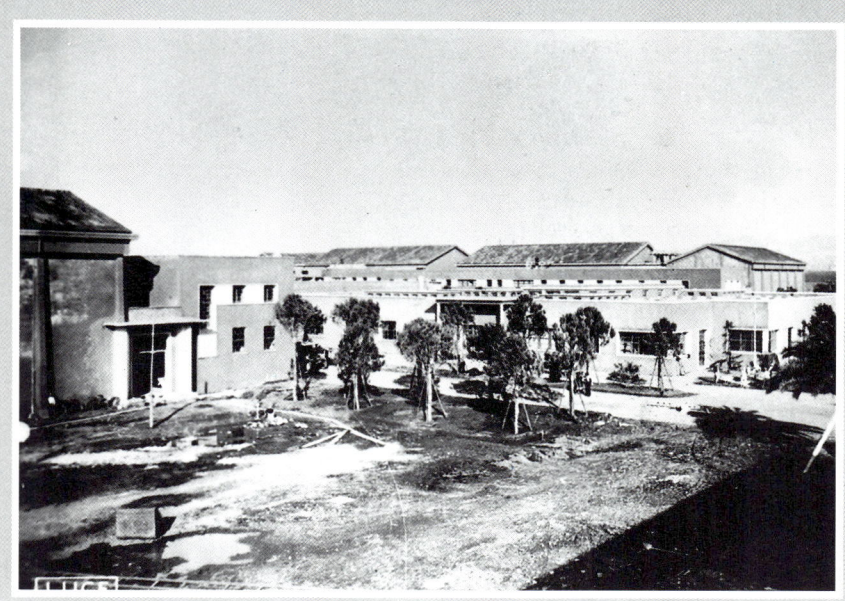

*M*ussolini performs the opening ceremony at Cinecittà on the afternoon of 27 April 1937, attended by high-ranking officials, children in uniform, workers lined up like troops, generals, and members of the Italian parliament, with flags and fanfares. A report in the Roman daily newspaper Giornale d'Italia *described the scene: "The Duce received a tumultuous welcome as he came into the great open space which forms the vast and impressive entrance into this film city. He then watched the beginning of the films* Elevazione, *written by Vittorio Mussolini, and* Aviazione, *which will be made under the overall direction of Vittorio Mussolini . . . The Duce was then present at the synchronization of the film* Scipione l'Africano . . ." *Mussolini's motto "motion pictures are the most powerful weapon" echoes a similar Leninist slogan.*

It was in one of those newsreels that I heard Cinecittà mentioned for the first time. It was in 1936, or possibly 1937. The black and white pictures showed Mussolini in black boots walking across what looked like a building site with buildings resembling aircraft hangars or warehouses. He could be seen striding along deserted streets, flapping his arms around, with a swarm of uniformed Fascist bigwigs in attendance. "Today the *Duce* has declared open the cinematographic establishment of Cinecittà. At last Italy has a complex of her own for the production of fil . . .," boomed the loudspeaker. In *Giornale Luce* (Fascist Italy's newsreel) we saw Mussolini talking to technicians in white overalls; Mussolini, hands on hips, looking through the viewfinder of a camera; Mussolini approving, nodding his large head to attest this fact; and Mussolini stopping for a few words with men and women wrapped in what looked like sheets that were in fact togas from a historical film, and exchanging both an ancient and Fascist Roman salute with them.

I do not recall being all that impressed, and the cinema audience as a whole did not seem too moved either. For me, the Fulgor in Rimini has always been the epitome of all cinemas – this is made quite apparent in almost all of my films. These days, in the foyer at the Fulgor, there is a large photograph – of me. There I am, just above the box office. And I cannot help thinking that when the audience has not enjoyed a film, people will fix my photograph with disappointed glares on their way out through the foyer and mutter something under their breath at me. Many, many years ago, the then owner of the cinema used to stand by the box office, convinced he was Ronald Colman's double. Actually, the resemblance was less than striking, except perhaps momentarily, at three-quarters profile with his hatbrim shading one eye, but he had to stand stock still and be holding a cigarette just beneath his chin and an inch or two to the right·with the thin column of smoke curling straight up past his face. He was aware of this, and so would stand

The ritual, style, iconography and grotesqueness of Fascism in Amarcord (1973). In the scene above, one of the boys in the film dreams he is being married to the girl he loves not by a priest but by an enormous portrait of Mussolini made up of thousands of red and white flowers. "This ridiculous susceptibility to a theatrical and infantile masquerade, the subjugation to a ludicrous power machine, to an absurd myth is the essence of Amarcord . . . Ignorance and confusion on a grand scale . . . To this day, the thing that still interests me most is the psychological and emotional aspects of Fascism, this sort of mental block or arrested development at the stage of adolescence . . ."

accordingly, hardly breathing, motionless, halfway between the main entrance and the ticket window. Behind that ticket window, on the other side of the little hatch, his wife dispensed the tickets while she breast-fed her baby, covering breast and baby alike with a voluminous shawl, from whence came sucking noises and, every now and then, shrieks of the kind uttered by toucans.

He used to go to Bologna to preview the films to be shown at his cinema a few days in advance, and when he came back, he would tantalize us. "Ah, I'm not telling," he used to say, and then, with much shaking of the head and a series of exclamations in a great crescendo, he would hint that while in Bologna he had witnessed extraordinary cinematic goings-on. "Does he get killed?" we used to ask him, all agog. "The idiot gets done in!" he would answer with a sarcastic grin which rather tarnished his Ronald Colman aplomb. We stared at him in awe, filled with envy. "And the Jean Harlow film then?" "It will be here," he announced with great authority, "for Christmas." "And Wallace Beery?" "The end of January. Possibly. I'm not sure if I'll be getting it."

One Sunday morning, from behind a curtain, I remember seeing him quite alone, sitting in the front stalls almost completely in the dark, quietly smoking as he looked up at the blank screen.

Then there was the wife of the local chemist. She used to come to the Fulgor for a rather more tactile form of entertainment, sitting through each film three or four times in succession, surrounded by an eager group of vigorous lads. Even we youngsters used to have a go, continually changing places with each other as we slowly edged closer to her. Never actually looking at any of us, she would calmly smoke, through the netting of her veil, pouting with her thick lips, her languid eyes fixed on the screen while our excitement mounted intolerably as we felt our way up her thighs.

I would like to make a film about the Fulgor one day telling the whole story of what used to go on in that little cinema. During the years of Fascism an entire generation was influenced and to some extent protected by those glossy images on its screen, which provided us with fascinating glimpses into a richer, freer, happier and more pleasant country, America.

Generalcine

Giulio DONADIO Mariella LOTTI
Lauro GAZZOLO REGIA DI:
GIANNI FRANCIOLINI

L'ISPETTORE
VARGAS SOVRANIA
I.C.A.R.

MICHELE MORGAN · MICHEL SIMON · LOUIS SALOU
GINO CERVI · HENRY VIDAL · ELISA CEGANI
C. NINCHI · M. GIROTTI · C. STOFANO · P. STOPPA · G. BARNABÒ · V. GENTE
È UN FILM UNIVERSALIA PRODOTTO DA SALVO D'ANGELO
FABIOLA
DIRETTO DA ALESSANDRO BLASETTI
DISTRIBUZIONE WARNER BROS.

la Lux Film presenta i quattro principali
interpreti del nuovo film di sua produzione

LA FORZA
BRUTA
diretto da
C. L. BRAGAGLIA

Juan de Landa
Maria Mercader
Germana Paolieri
Rossano Brazzi

di imminente programmazione

GIUSEPPE VERDI

Carmine Gallone
Interpreti:
Fosco Giachetti
Gaby Morlay
Maria Cebotari
Beniamino Gigli
Camillo Pilotto
Germana Paolieri
Lamberto Picasso

GRANDI FILM STORICI S.A.I.

Esclusivita E.N.I.C.

un'AVVENTURA
di SALVATOR ROSA

Interpreti: GINO CERVI · LUISA FERIDA · RINA MO-
RELLI · OSVALDO VALENTI · UGO CESERI · UMBERTO
SACRIPANTI · PAOLO STOPPA · ENZO BILIOTTI
Regista: ALESSANDRO BLASETTI
Direttore di produzione: LEO M... Produzione: STELLA

film di Alessandro Blasetti

La Corona
di Ferro

Interpreti: Massimo Girotti · Luisa
Ferida · Elisa Cegani
Rina Morelli · Nini
Gordini · Gino Cervi
Paolo Stoppa · Umberto
Sacripanti · Primo Car-
nera · Osvaldo Valenti

Regista: Alessandro Blasetti

Produzione: E. N. I. C. - LUX

VOLTI NUOVI NEL CINEMA ITALIANO

LA GENERALCINE PRESENTA UN FILM DI PRODUZIONE CAPITANI I.C.A.R.

FELICITA COLOMBO

UN GRANDE SUCCESSO DELLO SCHERMO
PER L'INTERPRETAZIONE DI

REGIA DI
MARIO MATTOLI

DINA GALLI
ARMANDO FALCONI

ANGELO GANDOLFI · ROBERTA MARI · PAOLO VARNA · GIOVANNI BARRELLA

AGENZIE:
BOLOGNA · CATANIA · GENOVA · FIRENZE · TORINO · MILANO · NAPOLI · PADOVA · TRIESTE · ROMA

The first time I set foot in Cinecittà must have been 1938, or maybe 1939. I was working for a newspaper and my editor, a tailor who never removed the needles from his mouth when he talked and in fact was a walking mass of hanging threads, ribbons and pins, wanted an interview with the actor Osvaldo Valenti. So one morning off I went to Cinecittà. I affected a very casual attitude to the whole thing, rather like Fred MacMurray in those films where he plays a newspaper reporter, but in fact I was very excited and lingered outside, staring in disbelief at the towers, flights of steps, horses, the grand, awesome costumes, riders encased in armour, and aeroplane propellers whipping up great clouds of dust everywhere, with the cries, shouts, whistle-blasts, the din of huge wheels turning round, the clash of lances and swords. Osvaldo Valenti was standing on some sort of two-horsed chariot which had very sharp blades protruding from its wheels, surrounded by a great mass of extras emitting howls of terror. There was a menacing atmosphere of chaos, but a harsh and powerful voice pierced through all that confusion, thundering instructions, like a judge passing sentence: "When you get a red light, Group A attack on the left flank! When you see the white come on, you Barbarians take to your heels! On a green, horsemen and elephants rear up and charge! Group E and Group F hit the dirt! AT ONCE!"

The tone of that voice as it came through the megaphone, and all the clearly articulated announcements I could hear, made me feel as though I was at a railway station or an airport during a major catastrophe. I was a little alarmed, and my heart pounded. I could not make out where the voice was coming from. Then, all of a sudden, everything went quiet, and the extremely long jib of a crane began to rise, climbing higher and higher, above the sets, above the studios, higher than the trees and the towers, up and up, towards the clouds, until it came to a halt, suspended amid millions of brightly dazzling rays of light from the setting sun. Somebody lent me a telescope, and through it I saw a man thousands of feet up in the air, on a chair firmly bolted to the platform of the crane, and wearing shiny leather breeches, a helmet on his head, and an Indian silk scarf, with

A film within a film: part of Fellini's Intervista. *These production scenes from an imaginary thirties romantic film show how the young journalist playing the part of Fellini on his first visit to Cinecittà views the world of film-making as a chaotic marvel. The fictional director is a tyrant, charismatic and revered.*

"Actually, I thought I wasn't cut out for directing films. I had no ambition to be a domineering bully, but I also lacked the consistency, the attention to detail, the capacity to work hard and above all, the air of authority." On pages 18–19: in another scene from Intervista *two painters work on a film backdrop.*

three megaphones, four microphones and about twenty whistles round his neck. It was him. Blasetta. The director.

My second visit to Cinecittà was when I was taken there by Stefano Daffinà, an actor of about sixty. He was impressive, smart and upright like a manikin in a shop window. I had first come across him in the bar below the boarding-house where I was living in those dim and distant days of the 1940s. I cannot quite recall if war had broken out then, but I think perhaps it had because, of an evening, the city used to look as though it had sunk beneath the waves, flooded in a marine glow of lights masked by blue paint for the blackout. In his herring-bone greatcoat and with a white woollen scarf round his neck, Daffinà used to sip slowly and deliberately at his cup of coffee, taking a fastidious delight in checking his reflection in the large mirror behind the bar counter. Every so often his lips would part into a wide grin, and he would smooth down the greying hairs on the back of his neck and make the very slightest adjustment to the tilt of his Homburg edged in pearl-grey satin.

The young barman's reaction was a morale-boosting ''Well done, commendatore! Tonight, he's more like him than the man himself!'' Then, to me, in a low voice: ''He's De Sica's stand-in, would you like to meet him?''

He introduced me as someone from the north of Italy who worked as a journalist. Daffinà calmly peeled off, one finger at a time, the yellow glove he wore ostentatiously folded back at the wrist, and said, in a clear, resounding voice: "You have come to the right man! I have something to ask all you journalists. Why do you never write a single word about the 'stand-in?' We make a major contribution to the success of a part. Look at De Sica, a great actor of course, even when he is silent, but it was I who invented his smile! He used to smile like this, see? So you couldn't see the premolar here, right? One day he looks me straight in the face while I'm fixing the lights for him to do a close-up and all of a sudden he says to me: 'When you smile, can people see your premolar?' 'See for yourself', I said to him. 'Does it show or doesn't it? It's gold, too!'" Shortly after that, there he was walking arm in arm with me along a completely deserted street very much the grand gentleman preceded by a little cloud of smoke hovering above his long cigarette holder.

"I live there," he told me, pointing out the only small window with a light in it in what seemed like a mountain range of huge dark apartment blocks. "Come in, just for a moment. I still have a little Chartreuse, the yellow kind. I'll tell you the story of my life and give you a conducted tour of my wardrobe." While we were talking, I could hear the drone of an aeroplane somewhere in the night sky, then, a very long way off, a siren began to wail, followed by another, very loud, almost immediately above our heads, and then another. As these warning sirens kept up their mournful sounds, cannoning off each other from different parts of the city which lay huddled there in the darkness under the starry sky, we said goodnight and arranged to meet the next morning at the tram terminus and travel together to Cinecittà to see just how important the work of a stand-in was.

On this occasion, however, the huge liveried doorman decided he could not let us in. Stefano Daffinà smiled at him in a considerate, good-natured sort of way, so that his gold premolar glinted in the sun: "Pappalardo, you old fool," he exclaimed, "you have known me for thirty years, this gentleman is a journalist, you are going to get yourself into trouble, they're waiting for me in there."

Eventually we were allowed in, whereupon Daffinà took off his raincoat and whirled it round like a cloak, revealing himself in full evening dress, which he wore with a remarkable air of self-possession. A couple of Roman centurions hanging about at the bar shouted hello, and a Red Indian in a pair of dark glasses came towards him arms outstretched and kissed him on both cheeks. "This morning," Daffinà whispered to me with the contented satisfaction of someone whose instinct forewarns him of things that are going to go wrong but about which he can do absolutely nothing, "we are shooting the ball scene. Have you ever seen De Sica dance? Poor thing!" At this point he motioned to me to walk on tiptoe as he was, because we were now heading along vast corridors which echoed to the sound of electric buzzers, and then large signs on the walls would suddenly light up, menacingly ordering "Silence." Daffinà came to a halt, bending forward with one foot raised, in front of a small door on which there was a large wheel to open it similar to the doors of submarines. He had to turn very slowly in order to open this obviously very heavy door just enough to allow himself to inch in sideways, holding his breath, till all that was left of him was one gloved hand beckoning me to follow.

Once inside, the church-like darkness was broken only by diagonal shafts of light descending from above. I moved cautiously, aware of a silence around me which was pulsating with rustling noises, subdued voices, thin whistle blasts, and then, without warning, the coarse cries and brutish yells of a full-scale onslaught.

The flying dinner-jacketed silhouette which, in that darkness, I could barely make out, had been joined by a couple of youths who were hurrying the figure away, as though he were under arrest, in the direction of a large semicircle of other dark, motionless figures, all of whom had their backs to me, round the edge of an area which was very brightly lit. This, then, was the set, the magical set, moments before the clapper board.

Moving very slowly, I had managed to get closer, but I could see nothing. It reminded me of when I was small in the main square of the village where we lived and a peddler had

*B*uildings of Imperial Rome (above), Elizabeth Taylor (above left) and the triumphal entry into Rome (opposite), from Cleopatra directed by Joseph L. Mankiewicz (1963). During the 1950s, Cinecittà was a Hollywood on the River Tiber: the Americans came to Italy to make their films because it cost them less – they were able to use some of their frozen assets there, benefit from the favourable exchange rate and from the inexpensive, commendable workforce who were particularly good at reconstructing the world of antiquity for historical or mythological epics.
On pages 26–27: the arena built for the famous chariot race in William Wyler's film Ben Hur (1959), a scene which featured six thousand extras.

attracted a large crowd around him. I was trying to see what he had for sale, and stood on tiptoe, then got down on my knees looking for a gap, an opening in that wall of jostling bodies. I could only hear the peddler's voice. He was talking to someone called Cipollino, who was apparently inside a jam jar, telling him to get out of the jam jar and introduce himself to all these nice ladies and gentlemen. But Cipollino refused to make an appearance, and so the peddler pretended to lose his patience and gave the jam jar a good kick before producing a fountain pen from his inside pocket and holding it up while he told everybody what a marvellous fountain pen it was.

I could also, here in the darkness of this film studio, make out a single, shrill, bad-tempered voice growing more and more angry as it cursed one person or another. It belonged to a man with pointed sideburns, similar to the ones matadors have. He was in his shirt-sleeves with his braces hanging down, with a black monocle on a string round his neck, and a cigarette in his mouth that bobbed up and down as the avalanche of oaths flowed out, and a spare cigarette tucked behind his ear.

"It is not enough," shouted this man, as little clouds of smoke continued to puff from his mouth, "that you agree that I can call you a fool! I want to hear you say it: yes, I am a fool!"

On a couch covered in cushions there was a very beautiful woman. She was nodding her head in agreement and weeping at the same time. Behind her, two men in white shirts went on combing her hair regardless, while a well-built girl holding a mirror tried to hold it in front of the woman's face while she sobbed. Dumbfounded and unable to believe my own eyes, I looked this way and that for Daffinà, hoping he could explain what I saw, and tell me why nobody was stepping in to defend this poor young woman who was so lovely and was being treated so badly. But for Daffinà himself, things were not going much better: he was standing in another part of the set, looking magnificent in his evening dress, while an assistant was putting a white flower in his button-hole, and some other individual, a short, stocky man with enormous hands and a celluloid visor over his face,

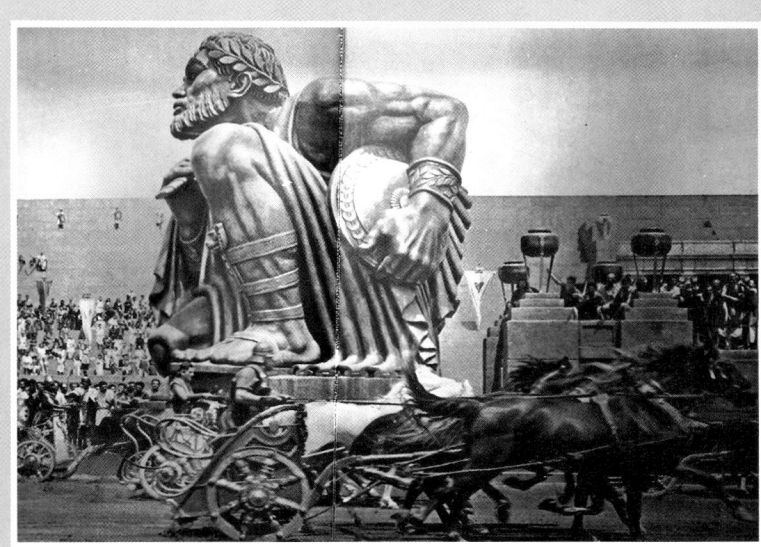

The present-day Cinecittà has to some extent been taken over by television and by advertising, both of which use the studios to make films for television and Italian and non-Italian commercials. Above: the entrance to Cinecittà and some of the offices, seen from inside Cinecittà; left: one of the many avenues flanked by trees; opposite: the sculpture workshops where craftsmen perpetuate the technique of reconstructing the ancient world. On pages 32–33: the figure of Fellini lost in the vast space of his favourite studio, Studio 5, the largest at Cinecittà and possibly in Europe, where he has made all his films from 1960 onwards.

was completely absorbed in slapping both sides of his face and shouting to someone up in the roof, obscured by the darkness, that the spotlight was supposed to center on him here, and when he said here, he meant here, after which he took yet another swipe at Daffinà, who responded to each blow with that famous broad smile of his.

Now the director was standing in front of him as well, looking at him in disgust, shaking his head. Then someone else seized hold of his elbows and pushed him like a wheelbarrow towards the actress lying on the couch, giving him a blow to the head to explain that he had to make a bow; this Daffinà duly did, in fine style, while the ever-present, loud, inebriated voice shouted: "Shall we try a take, dottore? Cue music!"

This command was repeated in turn by different voices, each sounding more threatening than the one before. Then, in a rare moment of silence, a cowed voice whispered: "Shall we call Signor De Sica, dottore?" The "dottore" said yes, they were to "call the son-of-a-bitch," and then added, no, it was not time yet.

Up above, the invisible spotlight operator continued to get it wrong, and Daffinà's face had by now gone all red. The face slapper shouted for someone to bring a dab of face powder, after which Daffinà was given another great shove towards the actress, who was lying with her head completely thrown back while someone administered eye drops and someone else nose drops, and a woman in a pink blouse sprayed bronzing powder into her hair.

The music started up again and Daffinà, looking satisfied and pleased with himself, waved to me to watch him dance, whereupon four or five voices yelled at him to get back to his mark, where the short, stocky individual with the celluloid visor had given up the slaps to the face and changed to heavy punches into Daffinà's back, because it was there that the five thousand watter was meant to focus on him and stay focused. Daffinà seemed delighted that the five thousand watter was meant to stay focused on him.

Two hours had passed and still nothing had happened apart from the continual shouts, music, slaps and tears from the beautiful signora. At last it seemed that somebody could

be sent to call Signor De Sica because everything was ready. I was a bit jittery. The fact that I was shortly to see De Sica in the flesh gave me a thrill of excitement. When I was a boy and living far from the big city, we used to regard actors as supernatural beings, and when on winter mornings, just before carnival time in February, they pasted up posters on the fronts of houses, inside the windows of the Caffè Commercio and around the piazza, with portraits of stars like Febo Mari, Gustavo Giorgi, and Moissi and the announcement that they would be coming soon underneath, it seemed like a gift from heaven to our poor, sleepy, forgotten town. Once, they even announced the imminent arrival of the De Sica-Melnati-Rissone company, and we counted the days as the date drew closer. De Sica's face, with his famous smile, had even been posted up by an unthinking bill sticker on one of the walls of the cathedral. The dean, the same one who had once stood in the pulpit and torn up a copy of the satirical magazine *Marc 'Aurelio* in front of the entire congregation, wrote an impassioned letter to the mayor and took it upon himself – only the sacristan would go with him – to go and scrape the poster off the cathedral wall. The great teeth of De Sica's smile refused to be removed, and remained there on their bit of poster for many months, keeping us company till summer with their gleaming whiteness.

But that day in the studio De Sica did not put in an appearance. There was an increasingly frenetic coming and going between the studio and the dressing rooms and then everything had to be put off until that afternoon. De Sica was unwell, "overwork" was the rumour whispered with respectful gravity, and the cast and crew began to break up into groups, with everybody talking about the Roma-Lazio football match, ration cards and buying meat on the black market. Only De Sica's stand-in, Stefano Daffinà, had stayed where he was, motionless in the big bright ring of floodlights, holding his gloves in one hand and still smiling just like that scrap of poster which had remained stuck to the wall of the cathedral, with the added bonus of the gleaming gold front tooth.

I was to meet De Sica many years later, when he had made

La dolce vita (1960) was the first of Fellini's films to be made almost entirely at Cinecittà. Opposite: the stars of the film, Anita Ekberg and Marcello Mastroianni, in Via Veneto. The enormous international success of the film made its title a catchphrase which evoked an entire era and which was used throughout the world as a name for restaurants, night-clubs and suchlike. Paparazzo, the surname of one of the characters in La dolce vita *became the international word for indiscreet, aggressive and invasive photographic journalists who had plagued the private lives of American film stars in Rome. Above: Walter Santesso playing the part of the photoreporter Paparazzo in the film, and below: the same character as sketched by Fellini. Top left: Fellini with Anita Ekberg.*

his name as a film director and I was trying to get my second film *I Vitelloni* (*The Young and the Passionate*) off the ground. Pegoraro, the producer, had looked at me with the imploring expression of the victim ordained by fate. "There is no big name in this film. You, Fellini, have just made one box-office disaster with *Lo sceicco bianco* (*The White Sheikh*). Audiences don't want to come and see Sordi. And Leopoldo Trieste, whom you stubbornly insist on using again, is a nobody! At least agree to having De Sica for that part. Talk to him, try and persuade him to accept the role, don't take me to the cleaners!" And he sat at the table with his head in his hands, sobbing.

So, one winter's night, I went to see De Sica, who was working then on *Stazione Termini* (*Indiscretion of an American Wife*). The appointment was for after midnight, in a first-class railway carriage on a siding which was a long way from any platform. It meant walking with difficulty over the wet ballast along the track; I remember the rails were slippery from the mist; and there was the continual fear that every gleam in the distance could be a train heading towards us. The little man in front of me talked to me without turning round, in a tone of voice which made me feel I was being led to an audience with the pope; he said he was going to climb on board first and take a look, because it was possible that the commendatore was asleep, in which case it would be necessary to wait for him to wake up. "I could throw a pebble up at the carriage window," he suggested. But there was no need for that: De Sica was still up; I could see him in the dark shadow of the first-class compartment, and with a welcoming air he beckoned to me to enter.

I had never seen him close up before. The velvet and silver charm of his personality had remained intact. Even the flute-like, slightly trilling voice was the same. De Sica, like Totò, managed to retain even in real life that soft, mysterious quality which made him seem distant and inaccessible like the image in the depths of a looking glass. He was very likeable, as though being likeable was his profession, his philosophy of life: be likeable, and much will be forgiven you. And De Sica was likeable even when he became the poetic interpreter of a country at war, an Italy full of destruction and wretchedness, and was obliged to adopt serious stances and tones of voice resounding with a bitter awareness of what was happening.

*O*pposite: during the filming of
La dolce vita, *Fellini giving the
variety artist Polidor some advice
for a night-club routine, and, on
this page, rehearsing Anouk Aimée
in the part of Maddalena. In Italy
the film provoked moral outrage
and hostility. At the Milan
premiere, some of the audience
hurled insults and spat at Fellini
and Mastroianni; and in a number
of churches in the Veneto region,
posters edged in black (the
traditional Italian way of
announcing a death) asked for
prayers for "the soul of Fellini the
sinner." In the Italian parliament
several different questions were put
down calling for stringent
measures to be taken against the
film.*

A scene from La dolce vita, showing the statue of Christ airborne over Rome and, left, a scene from the miracle, the imaginary appearance of the Virgin Mary to two children at the Santuario del Divino Amore, near Rome.

"It has never been my intention to chastize people for their morals. Nor is it my nature to be a moralist. Descriptions of La dolce vita as a reflection of the age, a merciless document that puts a whole society on trial, certainly didn't come from me. For me, La dolce vita is simply the story of the adventures, by day and by night, of a hack journalist."

I sat down in front of him in the dark compartment, where the air felt muffled and unreal, and rather nervously described the role I wanted to offer him. It was that of a great actor, I said, a great actor who had once been famous, but whom life had since compelled to make serious compromises and was now appearing in a live variety act which played in cinemas as a support before the main attraction. "One night, this small revue troupe arrives in a remote country town, where a young man full of dreams and literary ambitions asks the famous actor whose heyday is past to listen to a play he has written, and the actor agrees." De Sica was smiling in sympathy, approvingly, and murmured something about young people. Encouraged by this, I pressed on with my story till I reached the scene in which the old lecher reveals his true intentions to the naive young playwright. De Sica, who may have been dozing off for a fraction of a second, continued to smile benignly; suddenly the penny seemed to drop, and he stared at me in surprise with a worried look: "You mean that the actor had other ideas, something else in mind?" Then, after a slight hesitation, his voice almost hoarse, he added: "He's a fairy?" I nodded, feeling a little embarrassed. You could have heard a pin drop. "But," he said at last, with a serious expression on

Opposite: a scene from La dolce vita *with Marcello Mastroianni and Valeria Ciangottini as the girl epitomizing youth, innocence and vitality. Above: the discovery on the beach of a mysterious jelly-like, symbolic sea monster, which comes at the end of the film. "Several monsters were prepared, but I couldn't make up my mind which one to use: a great jelly-fish which was already in a state of decomposition, or perhaps a black sperm whale which had already been partly eaten by other fish . . . in the end I decided that this enormous, shiny ray with its small bright open eye was the most shocking."*

his face, "a nice person?" "Oh, very," I hastened to affirm. De Sica now started nodding his head as though in animated conversation with his thoughts, and nibbled at the inside of his lips; then, once again, in that fine melodious voice of his, he declared, "because there can be a great deal of humanity in them, more than we might realize." "But of course," I said, "there is no doubt about it."

Someone from the production crew then came in and announced in a rather servile manner that the lights were ready and the actors were wanted on the set. De Sica got up, adjusted the large scarf around his neck, and offered me his large, soft, warm hand: "Well done, a good character. I like it. Make an appointment with my lawyer. We'll discuss it. But don't forget: he's got to be humane."

For reasons which now escape me, it was not possible to engage De Sica, and perhaps it was better that way: the character he would have created would have been too likeable, too charming, and too amusing, and the public might not have understood or even disapproved of Leopoldo's bewilderment and flight in the scene on the sea-front at night, when the old actor, in a soft, inviting voice, persuades the young man to come with him to an even more secluded and remote place.

Sometimes I feel as though I do not know Cinecittà at all. In my mind it is really only a few pieces of scenery and one or two areas of the actual site. The first is the entrance, which has an aura of mystery to it that gives one the sensation of crossing a unique and enchanted threshold. More than most other thresholds or entrances, the gate at Cinecittà is a symbol. For me, it has represented a beginning. When I went in there for the first time, the gate-keeper was a real Guardian of the Threshold, a giant of a man well over six feet tall called Pappalardo who wore a great yellow robe which came down to his feet, trimmed with military epaulettes, pockets and insignia, and a hat with a brim bearing the word Cinecittà in raised letters.

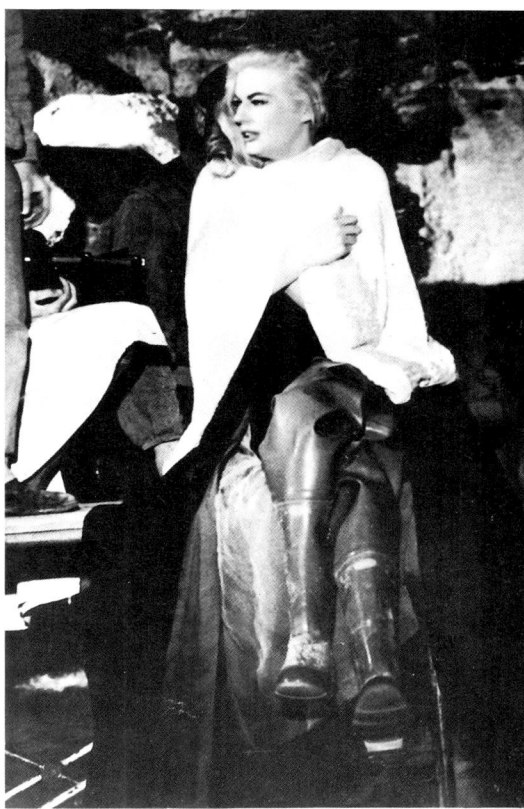

Nowadays the gate is guarded by a private police team in light blue uniforms, with pistol holsters and bullet-proof waistcoats, who sit inside a guard post full of closed-circuit television screens and protected by bullet-proof glass. The gate is operated by barriers which can only be lifted electronically. Vigilantes at the entrance to a dream factory, an amusement park, they add the dramatic touch which is typical of present-day society. They are also quick to advise that access to Cinecittà is not open to all, but only to those who belong within its walls.

Another part of Cinecittà on which I can speak with some authority is the bar. Again I cannot help making a comparison with images of prison canteens or station buffets, or psychiatric hospitals where patients hang around with no idea of time or purpose. Perhaps the bar at Cinecittà, when I think about it, could be most accurately compared to an old lunatic asylum, where mental illness is in the company

of its own illusions. And in fact you can see cardinals, revolutionaries, SS men, troglodytes, green lizards more than six feet long, and concubines, all drinking cups of coffee and eating slices of pizza. They buy rolls and sandwiches and take them out in plastic bags; I have even seen such snacks being stuffed into the pouch of a large kangaroo with the help of Richard Burton who explained affectionately to Elizabeth Taylor, who was more lost in wonder than alarmed by the huge animal, that this particular kangaroo was all wrong because its ears were too far forward on its head. She, in her magnificent Cleopatra costume, a mass of jewels and feathers, looked around her with those incredible violet-coloured eyes as though searching for the perpetrator of such a blunder.

When I worked as a scriptwriter, I used to spend hours on end in a corner of that bar which would not have looked out of place in a nightmare painting by Hieronymus Bosch, trying frantically to re-write the dialogue for the scene which the director was waiting on set to shoot. The actor and leading lady of the film in question had decided that the things they were being asked to say to each other were "unspeakable." Those characters would never have expressed themselves as I had made them do in my screenplay; and so with melodramatic urgency, I was collected, or perhaps more accurately snatched, from home and brought in to Cinecittà to put matters right.

With my portable typewriter on my knees, sitting at a little table littered with left-overs of all kinds, amid the bawling and shouting of people issuing orders and the yells of the crew leaders coming in to collect up groups of extras sprawled over the seats and the bar, I would make up new lines, trying them out to myself in a subdued voice, while surrounded by four or five pests making the usual complaints and asking me to throw in a line for them too and get the director to let them say it.

"But he'll listen to you," they would insist, pandering to me, "Without your talent, how would he ever earn a crust? He owes his success to you! Can I get you a cappuccino?"

Marcello

meches grigio argento

nitro lcom sul velletto reco comino

Truco fallito berlaces. Borsa di plastica vicimit di sabbia sotto glu occhi

spemo en cravatta rossa pieli in puma it sinistruso

I was saved by the assistant director pulling the sheet of paper I had just typed out of the machine and running off with it, followed by me, and the extras on my heels, still hoping for a bit part. One of these actors, on one occasion, was on her way out when she pretended to have an epileptic fit, shouting and kicking out like a madwoman and threatening to kill us all. The guards had to be called and they sent for an ambulance. The wailing of the sirens in the distance on the highway was enough to calm her down. Suddenly she was smiling and offering to buy everyone a drink.

My director's office is another of the places which represents a microcosm of the whole of Cinecittà for me. It is on the upper floor of Studio 5 where I have worked for so many years. It consists of one large room, dominated by a notice board which hangs above my desk and is covered in green billiard-table baize. Here, while hoping to give the impression that I have a thousand things to do, I stick pieces of paper with names, addresses and ideas on them, even suggestions and instructions to myself which are half an attempt at organization and half just clowning about: like the one reminding me that making a film involves dangers and uncertainties. But there is a time, at the beginning of a project, when that notice board begins to act as an assembly point for photographs of faces: smiles and grimaces gaze at the back of my head, forerunners of the features, types and characters which already tentatively belong to the new film, and which plague me until I finally have to include them.

At the start of a film, my office is like the enquiry desk at police headquarters, as my assistants make telephone calls to London and New York, making enquiries, searching for people about whom they know next to nothing; the file of photographs is continually being leafed through, and then it is discovered that of the possible candidates for a part, one is on the run in Latin America, another has had a sex change, and yet another, once an unimpressive twelve-year-old, has turned into a hirsute, sweaty youth doing military service. I want to see every face on earth: I am never satisfied, and if I see a face I do like, then I want to compare it with still more faces, with every available face. It is an obsession.

The fact is that the process of looking for faces, bodies, and gestures among complete "unknowns" allows the film to begin to take shape as never before. This is the most fascinating stage: the film exists in flashes, in bits and pieces. And I surrender to the allure of these flashes and bits and pieces, to the hundred or more different, even contradictory possibilities being offered to me for a single part. When I am in my office, the door opens and in comes a little old man or a countess, someone selling watches, a fat man or an exorcist . . . I see a hundred just to choose two for the film. But all the time I am comparing clothes, speech, moustaches and nervous twitches. One aspiring actor is thrilled because I insist on having his picture taken when all I actually want is a photograph of his glasses.

I have never decided to choose an actor because I am impressed by his expertise or his professional ability, just as I have never turned down an amateur because he has no experience at all. I am constantly searching for expressive faces, which have character and say everything about themselves as soon as they appear on screen. I tend to use make-up and costumes to bring out everything which may point to the psychology of that person. I have no system of selection. The choice depends on each individual person I have in front of me and how much I can understand of what is behind the faces of these strangers that I am seeing for the

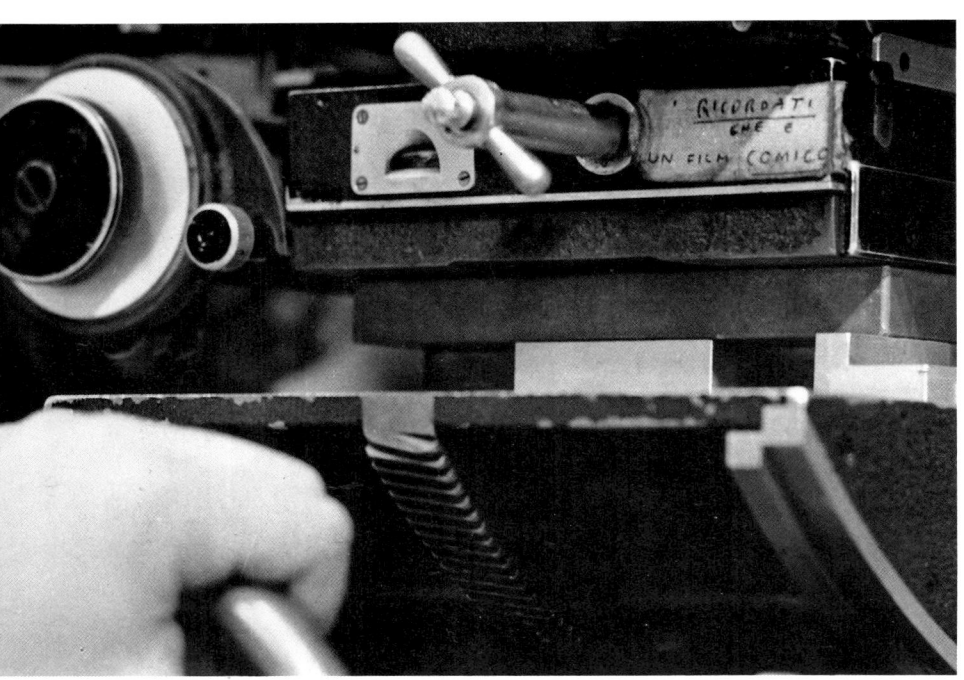

A reminder written by Fellini to himself and stuck on to a camera during the making of his 1963 film Otto e mezzo (8½), which reads: "Remember, this film is meant to be funny." "As it turned out, it wasn't as funny as I'd intended it to be." Opposite: two scenes in the harem in which the protagonist dreams of bringing together to live in harmony all the women from his past, present and future: above, the joyful arrival of the master of the house, Marcello Mastroianni (the actress in the center of the frame is Madeleine Lebeau), and below, the women he loves giving him a bath.

first time. And if I make an error of judgment, if for instance I look at a particular face, and its features, its lines, tics, grimaces and shadows immediately suggest a character, a type with a certain strength or charisma, and then when I take a second look, or worse still actually in studio at the start of filming, I notice that the face does not have those qualities, I do not despair, nor do I make a great scene about it, I simply change the part. I do not force the actor to take on some persona I have imposed on him, I just ask him to be himself. I prefer to get him to express himself the way he is able to and adapt the part to him. Most of the time I do not point this out to him, to avoid making him reticent, ashamed or resentful; and yet I could always say to the actors who are in a film of mine: "Just be yourselves, and don't worry. Let's try it together and see what happens. It will always work out, everyone has the face that belongs to him, and he couldn't have any other. All faces fit – life never gets it wrong."

Actors who think about the part, turn up with their own ideas, and have learned the script by heart, make me uneasy. Sometimes I try to explain to them why. What if I should want to change the lines, or think up a new scene, or suddenly make a different film, even change my job?

The work I do with the actors can almost always be summed up as a series of suggestions taken from observing life in general. One activity that helps me in this area is observing the actors while they are working, or making a phone call, or talking to someone about macrobiotic food or the age of a colleague, when they are having a meal, starting to get on well together or discussing politics, when they are chatting to the stage-hands about the perennial Roma-Lazio football match, it is there that I see what I want. I often find myself repeating the same phrase: "Do it like you did that time when . . ." That time might have been, for example, when they had an argument with a waiter at the restaurant. I can suggest to the actor who is supposed to say to his lover or his son, "Get out of this house!" "Do it like that time when you said to the waiter, 'This rice is over-cooked'." In fact, I sometimes go so far as to get the actor to say "This rice is over-cooked" rather than "Get out of this house!" These things can always be sorted out at the dubbing stage.

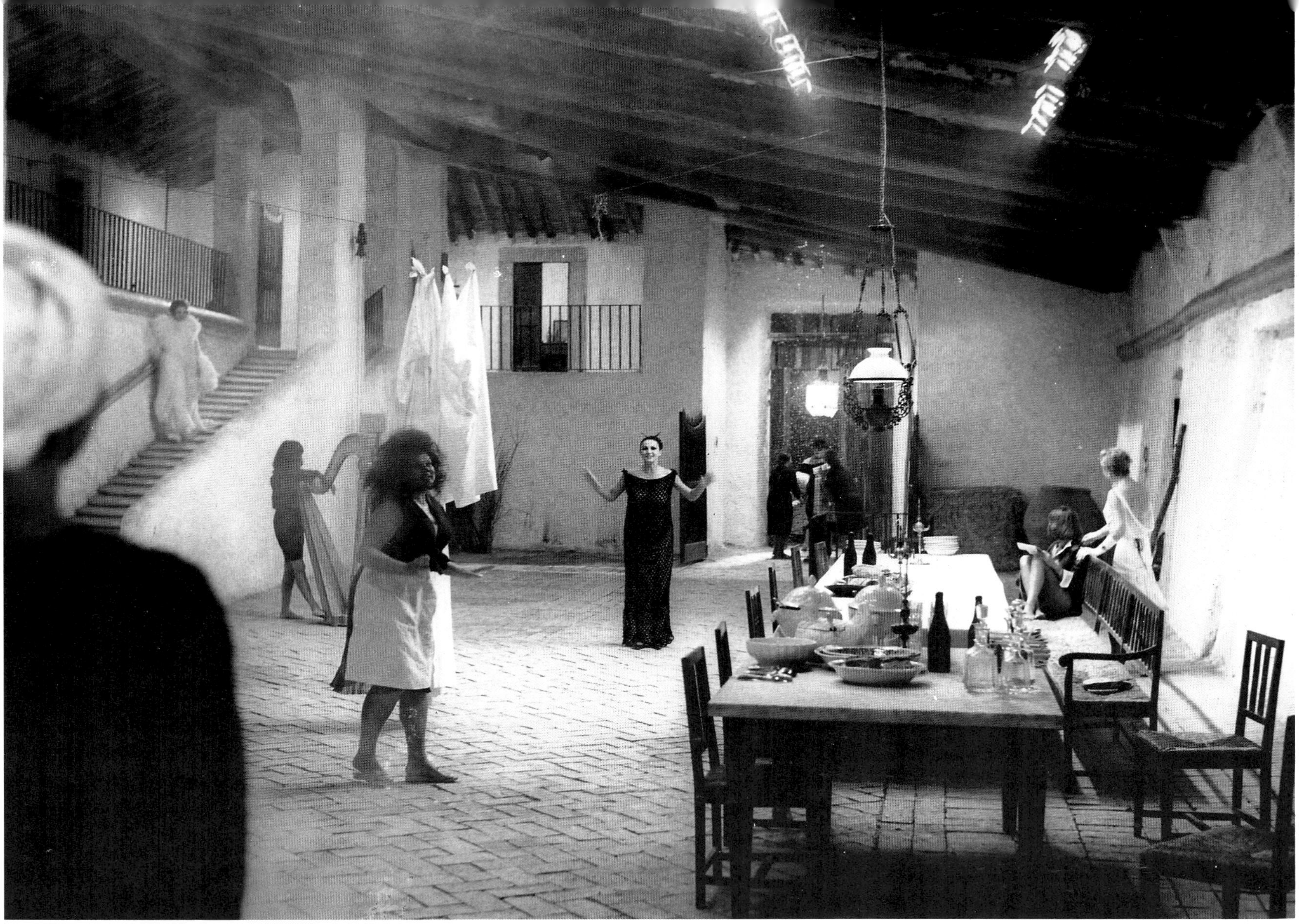

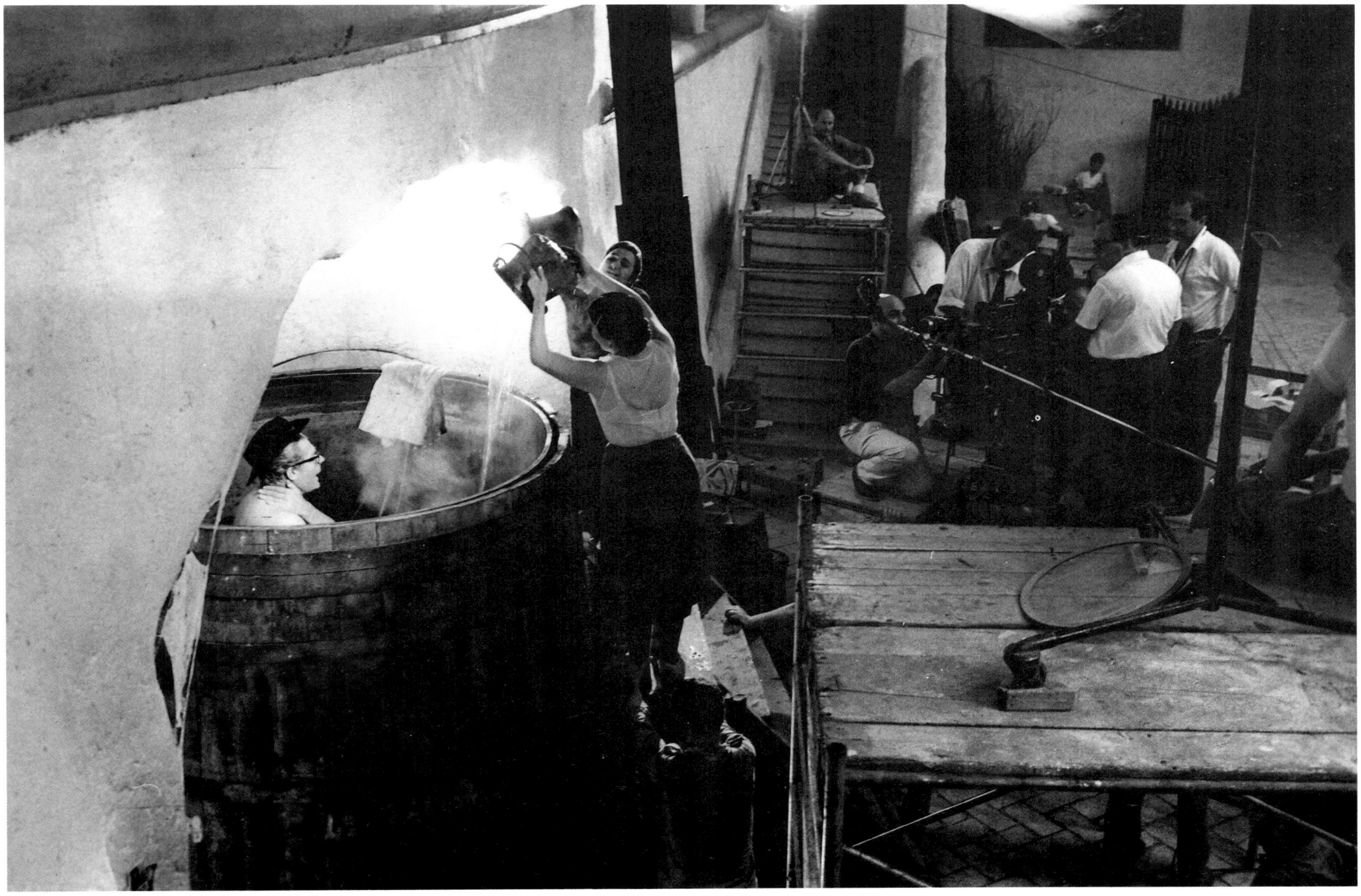

*I*n a scene from 8½, Marcello
Mastroianni stands in the foyer of
the Hotel delle Terme, where the
character he is playing, a film
director with a creative block, has
taken refuge. The actor has been
made up and dressed to look like
Fellini. "But it is not true to say
that Marcello is me, my film
double, my alter ego . . . I put my
hat on his head not to identify him
with me, but to give him a clue, a
hint; to create a channel for a
flowing communication of ideas
. . . I try to make him resemble me
because it is, for me, the most
direct way to see the character and
the story. It is a very delicate
operation, made possible only on
the strength of a deep friendship
and a shameless desire to
perform."

Underneath the large notice board in my office at Cinecittà, there is a desk of the kind that mediums use for table turning: it creaks, rocks, groans, coughs, is full of very sharp corners, with drawers which will collapse under the slightest pressure. On the desk are two telephones, one completely private direct line, the other connected to the switchboard. I always answer the direct line; its ringing never fails to intrigue me with the promise of something unexpected, the possibility of a surprise, or an urgent communication I simply have to know about. And while I am only too aware that ninety-eight telephone calls out of a hundred bring problems, unacceptable demands, ghastly invitations and outlandish requests from my journalist friends, curiosity always wins. It is the same curiosity which makes me agree to see people who are only going to get me involved in useless meetings from which I will try to escape; scroungers, pathological liars, deranged individuals. I make a point of avoiding social occasions, out of shyness and fear, to avoid having to please those present by saying the right thing and because I find myself ignorant and ill-prepared on all those issues (politics, sport, television, current preoccupations) that feed social small talk. And yet I cannot resist strangers. To go and have a look, to see and be seen, is an insuperable desire of mine; even when I tell myself that I should keep clear of anything that could distract me from the film I am making, deep down inside I think that somewhere along the line everything can turn out to be useful; even when I become unjustifiably irritated with someone who will not keep nuisances away, deep down I do not like the idea that the people I have got away from were maybe, who knows, interesting.

Next to the telephone on the desk in my office at Cinecittà, there is a statuette of Jimmy Durante, the American comedian: it was a present from the United States and it came wrapped up in an enormous parcel inside a large box. I have always liked it and keep it near me; there is no great significance in that, but it is amusing to watch the intense looks some of the visiting journalists give this figure of Jimmy Durante, as though they are searching for meaningful explanations, improbable parallels, some secret familiarity

Opposite: dream sequences from 8½. "I don't know if the thinking of Carl Gustav Jung has influenced my films from 8½ onwards; I only know that reading some of his books has undoubtedly encouraged and facilitated an exploration of deeper areas and has been an urgent stimulus for the imagination. I have often regarded myself as seriously limited by the fact that I never have general thoughts on anything . . . Reading Jung, I feel as if I'm being released, set free from the sense of guilt and the inferiority complex which this limitation has invariably caused in me . . ."

Above and opposite: stills from 8½; the grand staircase at the Hotel delle Terme where the Mastroianni/ Fellini character lives; the ghostly procession of bathers at the thermal baths; and the country cemetery in which the hero dreams of a sad reunion with his father and mother (played by Annibale Ninchi and *Giuditta Rissone). "My father was a sales representative, and as a child I associated the word "rappresentante" [representative] with the word "rappresentazione" [performance] which I used to read on scruffy puppet-theater posters . . ."*

between the two of us. On the desk there is also a green exercise book in which it is supposed that I note important ideas: as a token of their affection, my assistants buy me one of these at the start of every film, but I have never written anything memorable in them. There is a ream of extra-strong white paper, there are pens and felt-tips, for writing down the odd line of dialogue and especially for drawing.

Why do I draw the characters in my films? Why do I make sketched notes of the faces, noses, moustaches, ties, bags, ways of crossing the legs of the people who come to see me in my office at Cinecittà? Perhaps I have already mentioned that it is a way to begin to see the film head-on, to see what kind it is, an attempt to fix something, no matter how small and insignificant, which seems to me has some contribution to make to the film and is quietly speaking to me about it; I do not know, perhaps it is also a pretext for starting a relationship, an expedient to keep a hold of the film, or even better to keep it talking. This almost unconscious, involuntary drawing of doodles, taking notes in the form of caricatures, doing endless child-like drawings that look at me from every corner of the paper, automatically sketching sexually exaggerated obsessive female figures, the wizened faces of cardinals, the flames on candles, more bosoms and bottoms, and an endless string of further hotpotches, hieroglyphics, sharing the page with telephone numbers, addresses, crazy poems, income tax sums and appointment schedules; in fact, all of this graphic junk, an inexhaustible supply of it spread everywhere, which a psychiatrist would give an arm and a leg for, is perhaps a kind of trail, a road at the end of which I find myself with all the lights on in the studio on the first day of shooting.

One person who usually gets into a state of panic whenever, at the beginning of a film she is involved in, I get out my felt-tips and sheets of white paper at home the evening before and start to doodle, is my wife Giulietta Masina. I have not told her anything about the film. She has not asked me. She waits, trusting, patient, silently putting up with my own silence. She passes the time filling page after page of a school exercise book of hers, where she notes down ideas,

A scene from 8½; the little railway station and the welcome but thoughtless arrival of Signora Carla, (played by Sandra Milo), the hero's mistress. Opposite: a drawing by Fellini for the character of the mind reader who performs at the Hotel delle Terme night club, and a photograph of the actor Jan Dallas as the mind reader, next to Signora Carla.

situations, reflections, and lines of dialogue for her part. She will not let me even glance at it: "Later," she says. "It's still too soon. You tell me how *you* see the part. I'm not quite there."

So, having talked about it as little as possible, the day comes when I give her a sort of outline of a provisional screenplay. Giulietta refuses to express an opinion on this; she prefers to carry on writing in her exercise book.

The first tense moment comes when she sees that I have started drawing: the first little circle I make on the paper she knows is meant to be her face, and I am going to sketch in the characterization of the role, fleshing it out in a doll-like figure which will embody the features of the part. My method of drawing certainly has a natural tendency to caricatures, and gradually, as I amplify the character with additional strokes of the pen, I can see Giulietta becoming increasingly suspicious, alarmed, and ready to argue.

Giulietta is very resistant to my way of seeing her, which she probably does not regard as a result of my natural fondness for her or my experience of her professionally, but as an authoritarian imposition by a husband acting on a whim. As is often the case with actors Giulietta is unaware of how talented she is, she does not recognize it, she will not admit her real flair for comedy and does not want to accept that what makes her special is precisely that interplay of jesting and drama her clown face can express at the same time.

Giulietta, who is a true actress, wants to be the opposite of the role she is working on with me. Every time, she holds back and only gives in to it after prolonged resistance, as though she realizes she is giving life to something hidden in her nature which she had denied. She starts off by loathing the costumes, the make-up, and the looks of her character. On set she usually displays a rush of enthusiasm, a passionate outburst of generosity, whereas I find I am more nervous and more demanding with her than with the others in the cast. I want her to do it well straightaway. I am ready to put up with mistakes by the rest, but when Giulietta gets things wrong it puts me off. This is deeply unfair of me. The fact is that Giulietta's role comes to life in my mind very much

earlier than the others. It is as if she is not allowed to go wrong. Sometimes I want to say to her: look, you were conceived of before everybody else in this story, and still you do not feel perfectly at one with the picture we are creating, how come?

But alongside this energetic, cooperative, hard-working Giulietta, another Giulietta seems to appear who says no, which makes me sense the same bewilderment Walt Disney might have felt if Mickey Mouse had said to him, "I want to be Robert Taylor." This inexplicable diffidence of Giulietta's, combined with a spirit of humility, I see as part and parcel of an interpretation which actors generally attribute to the category of "clown," but which I regard as the most noble expression of the actor's art.

Since childhood I have always scribbled on any piece of paper within reach. I was also only a boy when I learned to type: and now, if I want to look as though I am taking down a quick note or dashing off a letter, I do it with two fingers on an Olivetti 22. When I was young, my father, of an evening, in his shirt-sleeves and waistcoat like an American journalist, and with a cigarette in a very long holder, in the light of a desk lamp with a green shade, used to type on a huge black Remington, glossy and impressive like the one the dancers in evening dress danced on in the ballet commercial at the beginning of *Intervista*. He used to write letters, and copy out orders. He was a sales representative, and as a child I associated the word "rappresentante" [representative] with the word "rappresentazione" [performance] which I used to read on scruffy puppet-theater posters advertising the farce "Mr Bean In The Underworld." So my father typed away, and I looked on, fascinated by the ring of the bell at the end of the carriage and by his skill; during the day, while he was out and the machine sat idle, I used to take the big lacquered lid off, insert a sheet of paper into the roller which usually got scrunched up and torn in the process, and bit by bit I tried to type as best I could, until my mother found me and made me leave Father's "study" double quick.

In my office at Cinecittà there is a divan I never sit on. Or at least only on the rare occasions when I have let myself be taken in by meetings of the American sort which the people

on the production side love having and I cannot abide: I cannot imagine why those who turn up have been asked to come anyway; papers are passed around, so are pencils and bottles of mineral water. Intimidated by all the bureaucratic efficiency, I commit myself to the most petty of requests, and can feel the wasted hours slipping by.

My office leads into a small dining room where we eat. I am not too keen on the all-noisy-chums-together school dining hall atmosphere I always find in the Cinecittà canteen. I used to prefer to spend my lunch break trying out the nearby restaurants. But it took up too much time, so it was decided to fit a small kitchen and dining room for me and the odd guest. I never eat alone. There is always someone I am working with, or a journalist, not to mention all the people I never manage to arrange to see in town and rashly invite to lunch instead; like the tailor who comes all the way to Cinecittà to give me a fitting, the wig maker, and the administrators of a great many opera houses whom I try to compensate, with a hurried lunch, for their disappointment because yet again I have declined to direct an opera for them.

I remember one time – it was about ten o'clock in the morning – a graceless, loud voice rang round my office. "Can I come in?" asked ex-boxer Ettore Bevilacqua. He had come to see how many guests there would be for lunch and what we could give them to eat. Irritated, I mumbled some quick menu. He took this badly. He was unhappy, he wanted menus fit for a king: partly to please his own personal guests, scene shifters and electricians he invited into the kitchen, and partly because he was afraid that if my guests were disappointed by the modesty of the meal, they would say uncomplimentary things about me and my films. He tried to object: "How can we? The Americans are coming, and all we offer them is an omelette?" Or: "And what if the minister comes?" "What minister?" I ask him. "I don't know, the Russian one, the French one, the minister, anyway, he came once . . ."

Bevilacqua had come into my life out of the blue. I was shooting a scene from *Il bidone* (*The Swindlers*) in Rome, at the

*T*he fantastical closing parade from 8½, with all the characters in the film holding hands in a long line, and the protagonist-director Mastroianni as master of ceremonies. The entire process represents the overcoming of his creative block. 8½ is considered to be the most autobiographical of Fellini's works, but, as in other films by Fellini, what is most autobiographical goes hand in hand with what is most objective, as truth and falsehood become two sides of the same reality: "I have to admit that even in my films recounting the past the memories are actually pure invention. But then, what difference does it make?"

Felice Aqueduct, when I was suddenly bent double by a sharp pain in the back. Broderick Crawford started pummelling me in the back to straighten me up. Bevilacqua, then a complete stranger, intervened, shouting: "Do you want to kill him?" Broderick Crawford put up his fists. Bevilacqua was a boxer and a boxing trainer. There followed a tremendous punch-up, which Broderick Crawford tried to stop at a certain point by producing a one thousand lire note, rolling it up and inserting it into one of Bevilacqua's nostrils. Bevilacqua then demanded the same treatment for the other nostril, and spent the rest of the day strutting about like a wart-hog with these two bank notes up his nose. At the end of the afternoon, he gave me a massage with oil, and cured me.

From then on, till the day he died, Bevilacqua stayed with me. First as a masseur, though the massage soon turned into a Caligulan torture, and then taking on the responsibility of keeping me in trim. He wanted me, on waking, to drink a glass of milk and eat a steak (I think he managed to get me to eat one once, although he ate most of it). Then he gave me a bath. Then he massaged me, complimenting me on how "firm" I was. "The Count," he told me, meaning Luchino Visconti, "is flabby." He ordered me to "breathe properly" when I was hurrying out of the house. He would come with me as far as the actual studio camera, and then went to supervise my lunch: he was deaf, intelligent, affectionate, industrious and witty, an Emiliano Zapata type convinced that he was an actor and deeply disappointed that I never let him have a part in one of my films.

F̲rom the 1965 film Giulietta degli spiriti *(Juliet of the Spirits), a film which confronts the subject of marriage and its crises. Opposite: Sandra Milo, who plays a triple role as femme fatale: "The incarnation of mortified womanliness in the female lead, which is projected into an exclusively sexual figure. A kind of love witch, a mistress of eroticism and pagan carnal divinity."*

Above: a Fellini drawing and, top, a photograph of the female lead in Giulietta degli spiriti, *Giulietta Masina, Fellini's wife. In the film, she plays a middle-class wife, brought up as a Catholic, repressed, dependent on her husband as a father-figure, and obsessed by the idea that she might be abandoned by him and be left on her own forever.*

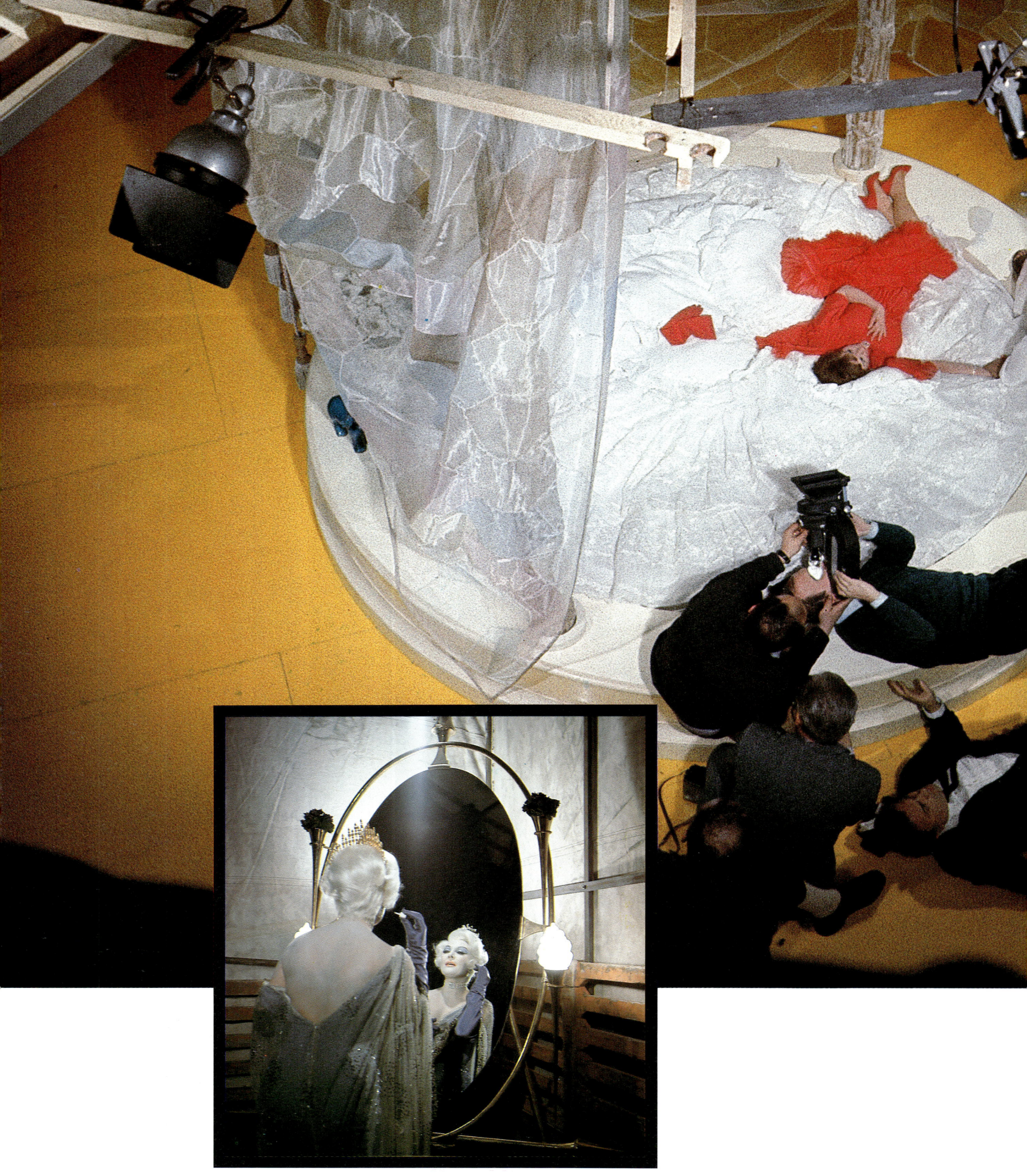

There are some days, the kind that make you listless and sleepy, when I can even get bored in my office at Cinecittà. I look idly out of the window, at the avenues below, and at the building opposite which houses the make-up department, and if I happen to know that Marcello Mastroianni is there, I can never resist the temptation to go over and see him, and enjoy the closeness and vitality of his friendship. Even as you go up the stairs to the make-up rooms, you are greeted by sounds of music and singing which get gradually louder as you approach, down the long corridor of dressing rooms with all their doors closed and the name of each occupant written on a little card. Sometimes these are the names of celebrities, international stars. I remember one written in pencil, stuck to a door, which read in dialect: "Nun so' nessuno" (I'm nobody).

The areas fitted out as make-up rooms always have their doors left open, and it is in one of these, with the din of radios playing, people talking, calls being shouted, the metallic crackle of the walkie-talkies used by the directors' assistants to tell someone somewhere else that they swear the actor or actress will be ready in five minutes, or that he or she is on the way down now, in the midst of the chaotic coming and going of dressmakers and assistant hairdressers, that I know I will find Marcello. He is underneath one of those great steaming driers that swallow up his whole head, clad in an enormous sheet that leaves only his feet poking out. I recognize him by the dangling hand bearing a cigarette that sends a trail of smoke up to the ceiling.

I know that under there, despite the great hubbub surrounding him, old Snaporaz is asleep. Eventually he catches sight of me in the mirror and raises the hand with the cigarette to say hello, hastening with his other hand to wave away the smoke he knows I do not like.

It invariably strikes me as odd that he is making a film with other people, not me, and that he is dressed as a pirate, or a gentleman of the nineteenth century, or has the full beard and moustaches of an abbot. It is all I can do to keep myself from butting in and telling the make-up artist to add a bit more dark to the eyelid, do something to a wrinkle or a curl,

or bring down the skin on his neck to reduce his double chin.

Marcello gets up, stretching his legs, and looks at me with the resigned smile of a convalescent, or a convict doing life. He puts out his cigarette, lights another one, and we take a stroll down the corridor. We have nothing to say, it is simply the pleasure of each other's company, like two school mates, or two soldiers on leave. He talks with his mouth twisted so that the smoke goes the other way, and we both say hello to Jolandona the dressmaker who is passing at that moment with a long bridal dress she is holding high off the floor over both arms, and hello too to Giusy the hairdresser, who we are both especially fond of, as she bows in acknowledgement, flattered and appreciative.

Marcello Mastroianni is a real buddy. There is an unpretentious understanding between us, a genuine friendship based on a completely mutual disregard for the obligations, duties and rhetoric of friendship. With him, being friends is not about ethics and demands; it is about getting on well together, feeling comfortable, sharing in the same jokes, tricks, playing with the same lies . . . He is a true actor. The way he does his job shows a psychological approach which I see as ideal and which is basically founded on trust: an intelligent, yielding, feminine openness to the character he is playing and to the writer's view of that character. Before a film, we chat for a bit, enough to enable us to grasp the fact that we are about to set out together on another journey. I tell him everything I know about it, and sometimes that does not amount to much. Marcello does not ask embarrassing questions: he arrives on the set with all the curiosity of someone who has come to see what is going on, and gives the scriptwriter the encouraging impression that the character does not know what is going to happen to him in the next scene – there is a constant perfect freshness about him, like the start of a new day. He instinctively knows how to reshape and how to understate; he is better than he thinks he is, and his modesty helps him to avoid all the pitfalls that can spoil an actor, such as vanity, being excessively extrovert, preening self-satisfaction, self-aggrandizement, and so on.

We originally got to know each other well through

*F*ellini directing the fantasy scene of the grandfather taking off with a dancer (Lou Gilbert and Sandra Milo playing the two roles). **Giulietta degli spiriti** *was the first feature film in colour to be made by Fellini: "I don't think I would have done this film in black and white: it's the kind of fantasy which develops through flashes of colour. It's a dream film in conception and structure; and the colour is an integral part not only of the language of the dream but also of the idea and feeling behind it."*

Giulietta: she had been in a play with Marcello and later talked to me about him. The character he played in *La dolce vita*, however, had not been conceived with him in mind. I wanted a slightly more sinister character, with a more mean and menacing expression. I had looked at so many actors, and considered several different approaches; it was then that I decided to see Marcello. We went for a drive. We talked like two little boys, telling each other things you would only expect to reveal after knowing somebody for ages, and we discovered that we viewed life and relationships with similar insight. There arose a great complicity between us. I made him lose ten kilos in weight (as I always did before the beginning of one of my films), and tried everything to get him to look more sinister: false eyelashes, yellowish pallor, dark rings under the eyes, black suit, black tie, a mournful look about him . . .

But it is not true to say that Marcello Mastroianni is me, my film double or an alter ego: in that case Giulietta Masina is an alter ego, as are Anita Ekberg and all the characters I have used, even the rhinoceros in *E la nave va* (*And The Ship Sails On*). I put my hat on his head not to identify him with me, but to give him a clue, a hint; to create a channel for a

*F*rom Giulietta degli spiriti. *Opposite: the heroine, played by Giulietta Masina, at the seductress's house. Above: a shot bringing together the two female archetypes in the film (played by Giulietta Masina and Sandra Milo), the Wife and the Mistress. "I think that for Italians marriage is still one of the fundamental institutions . . . The aim of the film is to give back real independence to the woman: any liberated man cannot do without a liberated woman. A wife must not be a Virgin Mary figure, nor an instrument of pleasure, least of all a housemaid: if a wife is treated in any one of these three ways, one ends up talking about something else which has nothing to do with marriage."*

flowing communication of ideas, made easier by the fact that he is already wearing something of the image to help him . . . I try to make him resemble me because it is, for me, the most direct way to see the character and the story. It is a very delicate operation, made possible only on the strength of a deep friendship and a shameless desire to perform.

Will I make more films with old Snaporaz? I sincerely hope so. The evening I talked to him about *La città delle donne* (*The City of Women*), though I had still not told him whether he would be playing the lead – indeed the producer was at that time insisting we should have Dustin Hoffman, and I have to say that I liked the idea too and thought him a very exciting choice – Marcello listened attentively but barely showing interest, like someone who knows that something does not concern him, but is bound by friendship and courtesy to look mildly curious. "It's the story," I was saying, "of a man who goes round and round women, looking at them from every angle so that he goes on being fascinated and terrified by them. It seems that he is looking at them without much of a desire to understand them, but rather for the pleasure of remaining lost in wonder and admiration for them, the pleasure of feeling enthusiastic,

disconcerted, and tender. Perhaps he is afraid, because he thinks that to find a woman, to possess her, means to succumb, to lose himself, to die. And so he prefers to continue to search for her without ever attaining her."

I felt slightly uneasy telling the story of the film in this way, rather moved; I went on driving, saying nothing, and Marcello too was silent. We avoided looking each other in the face for quite a while. And in that moment, almost unbeknown to us, the decision was taken that we would work together on *Città delle donne*.

"Cinecittà. Ninety acres of grounds. Twelve studios. Trees, roads, gardens, swimming pools and offices. Three hundred employees on the payroll. Technicians and craftsmen, sets and wardrobe, make-up artists and sculptors, editing and synchronization departments, a developing and printing laboratory: you go in with an idea, and you come out with a film. It is the most comprehensive film production center in Europe, and the place which most symbolizes the cinema."

This official information is all true, but for me the special fascination of Cinecittà lies in the air it has of being a dispossessed outpost, a hospital complex abandoned when it was only half-built, with its unsightly neglected meadows, the long hilly stretches of earth dug from the ditches where oily stagnant water attracts dirty grey clouds of frantic little flies.

I like exploring there, wandering about on those infertile mounds cleft by the hot sun, among great heaps of rotten timber, long sections of rail, and rusted or half-buried piles of pipes; there is grass everywhere, it covers everything, growing up the thick enclosure wall that runs round the outside of Cinecittà making the place look like a deconsecrated cemetery. On the other side of the wall, a battalion of large apartment blocks with millions of windows conjures up the image of a concrete army laying siege to a decrepit old fun fair and threatening any day to vault the wall and occupy it for ever.

Like an archaeologist who has forgotten his old skills and no longer knows what he is looking for, I stroll in and out of

Stills of Giulietta Masina from Fellini's films. Opposite: in a Fellini drawing and a production photograph from La strada *(1954). Top: in* Le notti di Cabiria (The Nights of Cabiria, 1957) *and above: in* Ginger e Fred (Ginger and Fred, 1985). *Masina and Fellini first met in January 1943 while she was working with a musical comedy theater group on Italian radio and acted in some of the radio sketches he had written. They were married a few months later, on 30 October 1943, at a time when Rome was occupied by Nazi troops and the atmosphere was oppressive and volatile. Fellini designed the wedding announcements himself. They have no children. Between 1952 and 1988, Giulietta Masina has had a part or played the lead in six of her husband's films.*

the papier-mâché ruins, as the wind lifts balls of polystyrene
into the air, and I might even come across the remains, the
left-overs from one or two of my old films: the gigantic head
of the deity from the Venetian lagoon, which I had made for
the opening sequence of *Casanova*, now lies slumped, one
eye missing, (it has fallen out into a puddle) while the other
eye stares up at the sky and four or five new-born kittens
tread precariously along the edge of its great eyelid. They are
watched by the mother cat, who lies stretched out on the rim
of the eyebrow sunning herself.

One time, I was drawn by the soft, sad sound of a flute
towards a landslip, where I discovered, huddled together in
a cane-brake, hidden from view in the midst of high grasses
swaying in the light evening breeze, three young men
absorbed in a cigarette they were passing around. In front of
them, a girl with a little crown of flowers on her head and a
leather jacket trimmed with fringes and military-style
epaulettes went on playing a soporific tune.

"We sleep out here," one of them told me, holding out the
cigarette to me, "the dogs don't come as far as this at night."
I accepted a puff, so as not to appear rude, trying to tell from
their accent where they were from. "We're from Holland," I

was told, and then the one who had seemed to be asleep asked me, without even opening his eyes, why I had never gone ahead with a film called *Mastorna*. He had read this in a newspaper back home, and the idea of the story of the film had appealed to him. I am not sure why, but this prompted me to attempt in my broken English to give this young boy I had never seen before explanations I had not even given myself to account for my having abandoned that project. Egged on by the atmosphere, the delicate lament of the little flute tune, and possibly even the cigarette, I said that the film, which I had had in mind for many years, had not yet inspired confidence, offered me its trust, or revealed its intentions.

"It comes to mind, however, at the end of every film I make," I went on, "as if to put itself forward again, and make me realize that now its turn has come. It stays with me

A drawing by Fellini and a still from Toby Dammit, one episode from the 1968 film Tre passi nel delirio (Tales of Mystery) – this was a film made up of three episodes directed by Fellini, Louis Malle and Roger Vadim. Terence Stamp stars in Fellini's episode, which is based on the short story by Edgar Allan Poe, Never Bet the Devil Your Head. In it, Fellini tells the story of a man who's in the habit of saying ''I'll bet the devil my head'' and ends up being beheaded by the devil himself, but makes it happen to an English actor who has arrived in Rome to work on a film. On pages 78–79: from Block-notes di un regista (A Director's Notebook, 1969), a sixty-minute feature for the American television company NBC, a photograph showing the huge buildings erected but never used for a fantasy film about death, Il viaggio di G. Mastorna which was never made, and Marcello Mastroianni who was to have played the lead.

Stills from Fellini-Satyricon *(Satyricon, 1969). Opposite: a production scene (above) and below: Ascyltos and Encolpius grappling with a robber (the actors are Hiram Keller, Martin Potter and Gordon Mitchell). Above: a drawing by Fellini of the character of Giton (subsequently played by Max Born) and (top right) Donyale Luna in the role of the witch Oenoethea. The film version of the mysterious fragment of a book which some commentators believe was written at the time of the Emperor Nero, and others date to between the first and second centuries A.D., attributed by some to Petronius Arbiter, and by others to a different Petronius, was*

Fellini's first historical film, and the only one he has made about the ancient world. "The world of antiquity is for me a lost world, one with which I feel no connection, it's a world totally foreign to me . . . Fellini-Satyricon is thus not a historical but a science fiction film. Rome during the decline of the Empire feels more remote from me than the Moon . . ." On pages 82–83: a scene from Fellini-Satyricon *that takes place on board the ship of the fearsome, depraved Lichas of Tarentum, with the sailors hauling in a huge fish, which is reminiscent of the final scene of* La dolce vita.

for a while, looks me up and down a bit, and then one fine day it's gone. I'm quite happy every time it goes: it's too serious, committed, austere, we're not on the same wave length yet, and if the day ever came when we were, it's anybody's guess which of us would have changed. I have my suspicions sometimes that it isn't a film at all, but something else which I'm not yet capable of grasping, possibly some kind of bizarre spiritual guide or pilot whose task is to lead me to new stories and imaginings so that when he finally bows out, there in his place will be the real film and without fail the one I shall actually make.''

Another time while I was walking in these desolate, neglected areas of Cinecittà in search of a stretch of thick wild vegetation where I could shoot a scene at night with Mastroianni being chased by some girl punks for *La città delle donne*, beyond the smouldering remains of a Wild West village which had been set alight by Red Indians from Iron Gorge or thereabouts, I found myself in front of a great wall, part of the Roman aqueduct, which rose unevenly out of a piece of ground largely littered with countless lorry tyres. I negotiated it easily enough, until there came a point, after passing a series of arches which went deeper and deeper into the ground until they could no longer be seen, when I noticed that in this wall, beneath a little porch cover of green glass, there was a small, well-polished door with bronze door knockers and a bell to one side of it with the words, ''Ring three times. Or four.'' I no longer knew which part of Cinecittà I was in, I had lost all sense of direction, and so I rang three times or four and when a little girl came to answer the door, I asked her where I was.

''What do you mean, where are you? This is the home of Pierone and family. Come in, sit down, Signor Orson is already here, he's having an omelette, we're all a bit deaf because of the bombing of Velletri, you'll have to speak up with my Dad.'' And it was not long before I had been shown across a cobbled yard where hens and ducks were scratching around quite peacefully in the company of two or three huge yawning dogs and into a cottage. It was a bit dingy in the large kitchen, but I could make out four or five people sitting round a big flame from the gas burners – one person

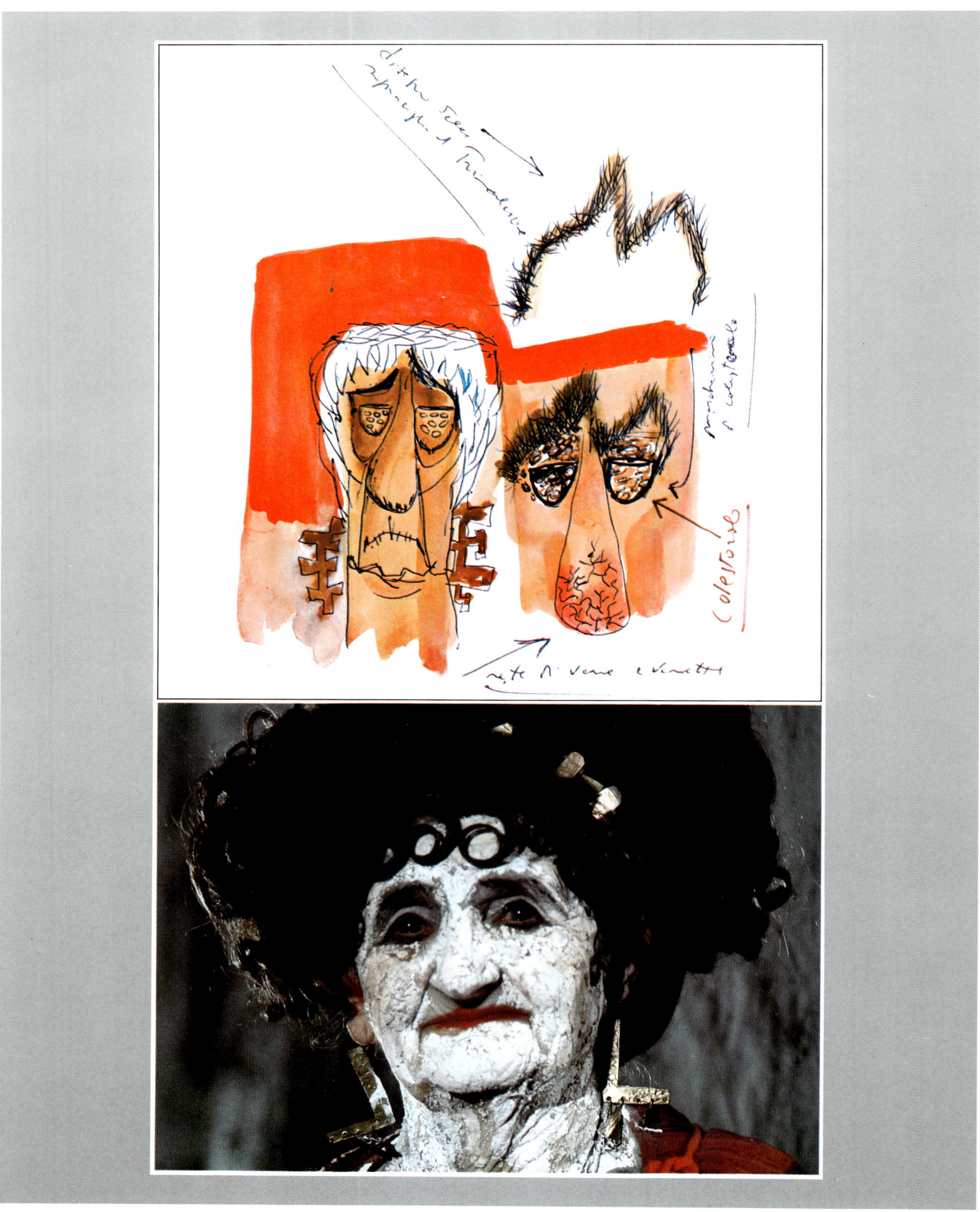

was huge, dressed in a black cloak which made the figure look even more immense. As I entered, this figure turned round as though in surprise and annoyance: it was Orson Welles. He was busy instructing Pierone, the deaf owner of this small mysterious farmhouse within the walls of Cinecittà, on the precise moment and the exact height at which to drop the egg yolks into the already beaten whites. He was speaking in English, though for Pierone, who could not hear anyway, it made no difference.

I am unable to talk about my colleagues, whether they are alive or dead. I become unsure, it feels like a fruitless task, talking about people who actually exist. I think the only people about whom one can speak with a degree of awareness and sincerity are made-up characters; in their case you can at least delude yourself that you know everything about them, but it is different with real people.

I found Orson Welles very congenial; I liked his physical presence, his size, the voice, that air of a king in a Shakespeare play, that proud punitive look of a drunken high priest of the Pharaohs and that solemn countenance, the archetype of the first actor ever, a protagonist through and through. The first time I ever heard him mentioned was shortly after I started writing gags for films by Macario and scriptwriting for several films by Fabrizi or Riento. Someone was talking excitedly about a very young director in America, a genius, who used the wide-angle lens and got not only his characters but also the ceilings of the rooms into his shots. My early unfamiliarity with the purely technical aspects of the cinema, coupled with my resolute lack of interest in lenses and focuses, prevented me from getting enthusiastic about this story of the ceilings. Then one day I saw a photograph of a young man with vigorous-looking jaw bones and flashing eyes who had written and directed a radio play that had terrorized America. From that day on, he fascinated me, like a character out of a picaresque story.

I'm ashamed to say that I have never seen *Citizen Kane*, nor his *Othello*; I saw a clip of *The Lady from Shanghai*, but the fact that Rita Hayworth was in it, whom I liked so much, and also that Gilda had been his wife, made me like Orson Welles all the more. You know, I think *The Magnificent Ambersons* is the

Opposite: a photograph from Fellini-Satyricon *and a Fellini drawing for the role of the wealthy Trimalchio, later played by Mario Romagnoli, known as "Er Moro," the owner of a restaurant in Rome. Above: another of Fellini's drawings, this time for the role of the actor Vernacchio, later played by Fanfulla. "I could say that ancient Rome in its decline resembles today's world, with the same mad rush to enjoy life, the same violence, the same absence of principles, the same despair, the same fatuousness . . . But rather than all these bright-eyed explanations, I prefer the pleasure of plunging into the unknown." On pages 86–87: the scene from* Fellini-Satyricon *in the swimming pool lit by candles for the ablutions of the guests invited to Trimalchio's grand dinner.*

only film of his that I have seen, and I liked it unreservedly. What a fine narrator he makes, sumptuous, rich; I was going to say "baroque" but I did not because I am not sure if this adjective might have a limiting, belittling, disapproving ring to it: when it is used of my films I invariably suspect that this is partly the sentiment behind it.

The second time I met Orson Welles was in Rome, when the legend of the man had been enriched by so many episodes, inspiring me to look up to him as an elder and more talented brother. He was at the Cesarina restaurant, a great dark forest of a man, broader than the entire round table for six at which he was seated. I went up to him, and with a regal sign of benediction he asked me to sit down. I watched the waiter bring him four first courses: minestrone, fettucine, cannelloni and rigatoni. He arranged the dishes around him, the way a card player lays down cards. He ate slowly, with the air of Henry the Eighth, or Jupiter as I had pictured him when I was at school. On another occasion, at half past six in the morning, out of the mist of a winter dawn over Fregene a great black jellyfish shape appeared through the pine trees. I then heard his fine voice: "Federico! I knew you lived here!" He was beginning to have trouble with his health, as a result of his many excesses, and suggested: "Federico, let's go for a swim, a run, and then get a

woodman's saw and cut down a couple of trees . . .'' We actually ended up having coffee. Welles was an adventurer artist, in the style of Cagliostro, Casanova, or Rossellini, with the additional intellectual qualities of the Anglo-Saxon cultural tradition. He inspired me with a feeling of brotherly solidarity, the way he would tour Europe like some warrior pope punishing producers and reducing them all to tears. I have seen so many of them, sobbing after making a film with him or pitiably euphoric as they prepared to do so. Welles was the great avenger of all the directors in the world who have been torn apart and driven mad by producers. I dreamed of being his right-hand man, conquering limitless horizons of cinematography, sowing panic and carrying out acts of vengeance.

It was always a pleasure to see him. He would fill your vision as elephants, clouds, or battleships do. A regal tramp, a man to sit up with all night and listen to tales of former glories when he commanded advancing armies, fought duels and signed peace treaties . . . He was a figure out of the nineteenth century: royal, priestly, and at the same time an outlaw. He had an air about him of grandiose failure, lack of restraint, debts and genial extravagance; he was a prisoner in a world too narrow for him, and all it offered him was the chance to advertise aperitifs with his King Lear voice.

I feel the same way about Cinecittà as I do for the circus. I identify with them and even feel directly responsible for them: as though I had invented them, it had been me who had put up all the tents and the big top and me who had built the film studios. So it can happen that I am called upon to do the honours on the occasion of a special visit, by a Russian minister, a delegation from Japan, or a couple of Swiss scholars . . .

Once, Ingmar Bergman came. He was supposed to be making a film at Cinecittà. The man in charge at that time was Pasquale Lancia, and I remember him, out of breath and ill at ease, asking me to come along on this tour of inspection. It was drizzling. Pasquale had a tiny little umbrella and a vast raincoat down to his ankles which made him look like an oversized priest of the parish church variety; Bergman who wore a short, shabby mackintosh and had a military haircut which tapered off halfway up his neck, walked along with his hands clasped behind his back, taking long strides like an inspector dreamed up by Kierkegaard or Samuel Beckett. He was in front and paid no attention to the running commentary Pasquale was mumbling under his umbrella. In front of the bar there was the usual little group of extras, walk-ons and electricians waiting to be called. In the face of Bergman's fixed and feverish stare which made him look like a medium in a trance, it was hard to offer any explanation for the presence of these individuals huddled together in fishermen's raincoats, having a smoke and a chat outside the greasy, steamed-up windows. What was more, Ingmar immediately shook his head when he was offered a coffee. So, as we stepped round the very extensive puddles, we saw the enormous, squalid buildings of the different studios going by as though on a dolly: and then Bergman, quite out of the blue, asked to see the toilets. Pasquale Lancia glanced at me with the look of a desperate man: in Italy it is difficult to imagine any toilet in a public building eliciting favourable comments, but the toilets at Cinecittà were actually inexcusable. It was raining in there as well; and in that desolate panorama of dilapidated corridors and chipped doors, we heard a voice, a not very pleasant voice emanating from

A̅bove: a scene from I clowns.
*Opposite: Fellini making up as a
clown for a photograph to appear
on the front cover of the American
magazine* Newsweek. *This
investigation into the clowns of
yesteryear is the first of Fellini's
full-length features to be produced
in conjunction with television
which, from 1979, became the*

*ongoing producer, co-producer or
financer of his work. ''The circus is
not only a show; it's a life
experience. It's a way to travel
through one's own life . . . The
spectacle of the circus, despite
being openly at odds with today's
world in some respects, must be
preserved, it is still of great
value.''*

one of those cubicles and singing to an accompaniment of unmistakable noises. In order to salvage a situation already as seriously compromised as this, I had the idea of suggesting to Pasquale Lancia that we visit the swimming pool. So there we stood in front of that concrete shipwreck, that landscape of ruins, something like a scene from *The Fall Of The House Of Usher*. Beneath the light rain which was now drizzling in earnest, all of a sudden Bergman came up to me and pointed with his very long finger at a corner of the pool where, underneath the veil of stagnant water puckered by the raindrops, you could see a host of small shapes, like a Sumerian alphabet, swirling about at great speed, like bacteria. Bergman had crouched down on his heels and was talking about tadpoles with a contented smile.

Pasquale Lancia backed away discreetly, so as not to disturb the private conversation of the two film-makers; however, every now and again, he did ask me to tell Bergman that the Cinecittà swimming pool was the biggest in the world, that you could do anything in it, naval battles, dolphin race, shipwrecks. "The Americans can't believe their eyes when they see it. Tell him that!"

But I would rather have told Bergman that, for me, those tadpoles which so fascinated him were the films I had not made. Luckily, some sort of embarrassment or modesty stopped me from opening my mouth, because I would also have had to tell him about a recurring dream I always have with unfailing regularity whenever I start work on a film.

The dream's setting hardly ever alters: it is an airport or a station, or the estuary of a river flowing out into the sea, and the action almost always takes place on the runway, or on the decks of ships which are about to cast anchor, or on trains on the point of drawing away from the platform. The meaning of the setting is patently clear, although in another version it happened that we were all already on board the plane and ready to leave, when the captain, giggling, announced over the loudspeaker that he had no fuel and we would all have to get out and push. This we all did, and I was urging those who were being half-hearted about it to put in more effort, but the whole thing was complicated by the fact that the wheels of the undercarriage were heading

off the runway into a field, and the plane turned round on itself, so that its nose was pointing in the opposite direction from that required for take off.

It was all too easy to interpret: I did not have enough energy to get the film I was planning off the ground.

Another time – here I am talking about the most marvellous film I had ever imagined and written – the aeroplane in the dream took off like a rocket, and the airport swarmed with people applauding enthusiastically. Except that, while we were already climbing through the clouds, the voice of the stewardess came over the loudspeaker informing passengers that the captain, I do not remember his name, was very sorry to have to announce that the plane had no undercarriage and so we would not be able to land at any airport anywhere. He regretted this, and wished us a comfortable flight even if our destination was now unknown.

And in fact that same film, which, I assure you, I liked enormously (look at all the applause at the airport) never landed anywhere, had no destination, in other words I never made it.

I could tell you the story of so many dreams like this, at least one for each film, whether it was eventually made or not, but what I wanted to tell Bergman was something else: I had imagined that I had once been submerged in the Cinecittà swimming pool wearing a diver's or frogman's suit, and discovered, down there on the bottom of the pool, all the dream-aeroplanes in a row, some with lights in all of their windows, others in darkness, falling apart, the wings fallen off and rotting in the water. On the cockpit of one plane I thought I read a name, "Mastorna," but I don't know if this was a real dream or whether it was a figment of the imagination which was also to be used as the opening of a film.

"Perhaps he doesn't know that the pool can be emptied and refilled by electric pumps in forty-five minutes!" begged Pasqualone Lancia while Bergman continued to stare at the tadpoles darting about all over the place in a burst of activity. I no longer knew what to say to him, not least because I had noticed he was now observing me in an openly questioning way – perhaps he wondered at my silence, or maybe he wanted to ask me just what we two were doing, strangers to

each other, crouching on our heels in the rain, against that background of desolation and decay. He seemed almost to be blaming me for the absurdity of the whole situation. That stare, which allowed for no appeal, no explanation, and gave me the impression that he was looking straight through me, reminded me of Paul VI, who, at the time I met him, had not yet become pope and was simply Monsignor Montini, Archbishop of Milan.

The Jesuits of San Fedele in Milan had defended *La dolce vita* in one of their journals, and this expression of consensus had been very severely punished: the San Fedele group was disbanded, the Father Superior was sent to Bangkok and Father Taddei, author of the review of the film, received an interdict forbidding him from writing about the cinema for twenty-five years. Feeling slightly guilty and disconcerted, I asked for a meeting with Monsignor Montini so as to attempt to speak on the Jesuits' behalf. The appointment was postponed four times. Finally I was received at the archbishop's palace, and shown into an enormous hall which was very faintly lit, so dark that I had little idea of where I was. There was some dim light coming from a small lamp on the desk. I had been told not to step forward until I was explicitly invited to do so. Montini came out from

behind the desk, and kept at a considerable distance from me. In such solemn surroundings, I could no longer remember what I wanted to say, but I tried nevertheless, making a great effort, to speak. I said that I did not mean to interfere, but that I felt under an obligation, on a human level . . . I am not sure, I do not remember now. Montini did not utter a word. He listened, without ever looking me in the face. At the end he said: "I shall pray that God enlightens you." To say goodbye, I went up to kiss the hand of the future pope and at last saw his eyes looking at me with the innocent detachment of a being on another plane altogether.

Only once have I included the pope in one of my films. Actually, there was a second time, in *Casanova*, but that involved an easy-going, tolerant, friendly, almost maternal pope, just the sort that Casanova would have hoped to meet in order to win eternal absolution.

In *Roma*, however, it was different. I had imagined a vast room plunged into darkness with a small amount of light provided by shimmering candle flames. Here princes and princesses of the papal nobility of Rome attended a show of magnificent ecclesiastical fashions. Organ music accompanied the appearance of monks, friars, bishops and

Drawings by Fellini and stills from the brothel sequence in Roma. *In the center of the lower photograph is the actor Peter Gonzales who plays the part of the eighteen-year-old Fellini. Brothels were closed down and abolished in Italy in 1958 – this scene is set in the 1930s. ''Those who used to visit brothels wanted to remain attached for as long as possible to an unstinting maternal figure who would take away their doubts and also their responsibilities, and who above all would not cause them problems . . . This return to the womb, which the brothels' clients used to act out with the regularity of a ritual, enabled them to put off the evil day, postpone indefinitely their coming to maturity.''*

cardinals, and their dignified, priestly progress down a long, horseshoe shaped catwalk which emerged from the darkness only to lead back into it. This parade of ecclesiastics, wearing sacramental robes which were increasingly splendid and luxuriously trimmed with silk and rainbow-coloured satin, took place amid the heady smoke of incense, while the voice of the announcer became more and more tremulous and agitated as he described these dazzling, majestic bishops and cardinals in their vast red robes and very tall miters, weighed down with necklaces, diamonds and rings. Some were very tall and emaciated, others short, and stocky, bloated out by all their ornaments.

The sequence, which was purposely extravagant in its choreographic pomp and exaggerated theatrical ritual in order to suggest a pharaonic vision of power and glory, culminated in a kind of apotheosis with the appearance of the pope, seated on a gleaming throne of gold and jewels. The hyperbole and excess are the fulfilment, albeit in this sumptuous way, of a satirical vision taken to its extreme.

But then something mysterious and unintentional in the atmosphere seemed to neutralize the whole irreverent show. The company was a Roman cinema troupe, characterized by the most perfect combination of autocratic arrogance and lethargic scepticism that, owing to its fundamental insensitivity, would never be affected by the sight of either catastrophes or miracles. At the moment of the pope's appearance, which was staged as a kind of immaculate, radiant epiphany, framed by a great piece of shining gold lace work and set against a dazzling wheel that sent out rays of the most intense light behind him, the group slowly fell silent. There were only muffled voices and whispers. But there was also a change of gear in the studio, an impalpable current of excitement. The make-up staff, who had climbed up on steps to be on a level with the face of the character I had chosen to play the pope (a versatile actor from Naples), moved about so slowly they were like underwater swimmers, uttering only the essential words and applying the final touches of white round the eyes, on the

eyelids or along the bony protuberance of the pointed nose similar to that of Pius XII; and in the presence of that waxen, pallid, ascetic face, which had been made to look incorporeal in all that light as though the flesh and blood of it was beginning to dissolve in waves of light, energy and spirit, I too, without realizing it, had lowered my tone of voice as I talked the actors through the sequence and directed the shots. Towards that Neapolitan playing the pontiff, up there in the midst of all those bright lights, I behaved with a deference which came to me naturally, offering him submissive suggestions rather than orders, as though I was no longer in a studio surrounded by the familiar faces of my regulars, but in a place of worship where one did not raise one's voice, out of respect for the sanctity of the presences there. So priestly and inaccessible was the figure of the pope, so sumptuously and terribly regal, that it had the mysterious power of the archetype, subjecting us to a kind of hypnotic, magical force in this illusion. The effect was stronger than the actual knowledge that it was us creating it, putting it across, bringing it to life. The producer stood there, eyes bright with emotion, and as the organ chords

*S*et designs from Roma, for a Roman street in a district built at the time of King Umberto I where people in festive, greedy and ferocious mood are dining in the open air; and (left) the scene in the film. "There are male cities and female cities. Rome is female, she is a magnificent woman, in fact she's a whole series of women. There's the maternal woman, and the mistress. Sometimes she's as fresh as a little girl, sometimes gloomy, sullen and bad-tempered. Elusive, impossible to define. Irritating, listless. A city like Rome can at one and the same time be any age and every age, wear any face and every face . . ."

grew louder and more overwhelming, and the lights sparkled and the great fans were held aloft, I heard him murmur: "Get down, on your knees." On his throne, the pope lifted his arms out wide and on his thin, cadaverous face, there was a pious and triumphant smile.

This scene enchanted and amused Luis Buñuel. "I would so love to have played one of the cardinals!" he declared with a smile, "Why didn't you ask me?" On the other hand, Anna Magnani felt disturbed by the pope in *Roma*. She saw the film when it was almost finished, liked it very much, clapped like a little girl, but the appearance of the pontiff made her feel disconcerted and uneasy. When I called at her house to ask her to appear in the closing scene of the film, I found her curled up on a sofa, dressed all in black, with a dark look like some gipsy queen, and very diffident. She wanted to know who else would be appearing at the end of the film, how long her appearance would last, what she would have to say, and why, in what way, with what nuance . . . She wanted to know everything, down to the last detail; she was always afraid of being made a fool of. She had the inferiority complex of a displaced person, all because of this fastidious approach to acting: in demanding unduly precise explanations and details, an actor is reacting instinctively to the thought of being used passively, and Magnani had become ever more diffident as the years went by.

I began to tell her, making a few suggestions: "After the scene in Trastevere, you appear at the window like an icon, an empress of the night . . ." She did not like that. "What do you mean, icon, which empress . . ." So, I tried another approach: "The camera comes into a crowded, noisy trattoria in Rome, goes along a passage and out into a small courtyard rather like a cloister, where you are having dinner with your closest friends, and, accompanied by a guitar, you sing a Roman song . . ." No way. "That stinks." Third suggestion: "A large, black, shiny, somber limousine, the sort cardinals ride in, is driving slowly through the crowds;

From Roma, *a drawing by Fellini and a triumphal robe for the pope in the ecclesiastical fashion show sequence. "I like the choreography of the Catholic church. I like its unchanging, hypnotic performances, the elaborate stagemanship, the solemn chants, the catechism, the election of a new pope, and the grandiose trappings of death. The church's merits are those of any product of the mind which aims to protect us from the voracious magma of the unconscious . . . And then there is the fact that I feel dazzled and captivated by the Catholic church, which has afforded the most extraordinary stimulus to artists, a vigilant and generous patron of masterpieces . . ."*

the people draw closer, crane their necks to see; inside it is you with your dogs, and you respond to their curiosity with a distant, regal look.'' Nothing doing. ''What are you talking about? Well, it's better than the other rubbish, I suppose . . .'' In the end I said to her: ''All right, the film is over, the camera catches you by surprise at night at the door of your house, I call out to you, I say a few words to you, that you are the symbol of Rome, she-wolf and vestal virgin, I ask you to say something about the city; you tell me to get lost and slam the door in my face.'' She liked that one. But not enough to dispense with her final objection: ''But I want to see it written down, understood?''

On the day we shot this little scene, I was moved by how excited and nervous she was. I had known her for a long time, and she made me feel small and ill at ease. Her overbearing, argumentative, foul language embarrassed me, and I did not know how to react. Then she would have agonizing flashes of humanity, and be maternal, sisterly. She was arrogant, defensive and aggressive, but underneath you sensed the despair of the evacuee or the deserter. Anna Magnani's charisma did not only come from her being the symbol of working-class Roman motherhood, laced with the drama and emotional blackmail found in all stereotypes representing common behavioural patterns; she had something absolutely her own, something magnificent. She was an excellent comic actress, but, like so many, she eschewed comedy. The meeting between the prostitute Cabiria and the film star Amedeo Nazzari which was later put into my *Le notti di Cabiria* (*The Nights of Cabiria*) was an episode I had written especially for her. I went to talk it over with her. I tried to tell it the best I could; she listened, pointedly examining her nails; Rossellini was alarmed, and attempted to modify and lighten the story line. At the end she blew up: ''And I get shut in the toilet by some shitty actor?'' And she told us both to go to hell. So then I wrote *Il miracolo* (*The Miracle*) for her, the story of a shepherdess who is made

A scene from Roma, *in which the cardinal – seated here in the palace of a Roman prince in the company of the aristocrats of the Vatican nobility – presides over the ecclesiastical fashion show. Opposite: a drawing made by Fellini for this scene. "I think I'm religious by nature, because the world, and life, seem to me to be swathed in mystery. And even if I had not been fascinated ever since my childhood by this mystical feeling which is projected on to existence and makes everything unknowable, I think that the profession I am in would naturally have brought me to a feeling for religion . . ."*

A drawing by Fellini of the Rex, the huge transatlantic liner featured in Amarcord *(1973), the film in which he recalls his birthplace and early years. The whole town is out in makeshift craft to see her off as she sets sail for the high seas. Opposite: a production shot of the Rex. The steamer never went to sea, but was painted on to the great wall in the swimming pool at Cinecittà, while* a system of tubes and pumps in the pool simulated the ship's wake. Outside the pool, boats, rafts, small craft and all the well-wishers, spellbound by the almost dream-like apparition of the Rex, were standing on platforms which had been fitted with wheels and mounted on tracks, so that with the aid of ropes they could be made to move, creating the impression that the ship was moving.*

pregnant by a tramp (played by me in the film) and who thinks she has met Saint Joseph. "Now you're talking," she remarked, satisfied. The mystical bit appealed to her.

Working in films brings people close together, and a unit, while temporary, becomes a close-knit community, with its own way of speaking, its shared experiences, conflicts, and its private jokes which nobody else can understand. "Tinted dawn," for example, was the catch phrase in my *Luci del varietà* (*Variety Lights*). While we were waiting for the "tinted dawn," in the stables of a large farmhouse where we had gathered, Peppino De Filippo told us stories about his childhood in Naples, fabulous stories of brilliant actors of a legendary kind that can no longer be found. We listened spellbound, as this wonderful comedian got a real kick out of the stories himself, doing all the wicked, sneering looks of the phony, brazen people he was impersonating; until someone on the production side rushed outside and then came in shouting: "The tinted dawn. It's come. Get out there. It's the tinted dawn."

So it was called "tinted dawn" in the screenplay, and everybody, including the most artless member of the unit picked up this rather literary expression and used it. For days on end, they would shake their heads with exaggerated concern and say to Lattuada and me, "Can't you see, even this morning we cannot have this tinted dawn? Last month there was no end of tinted dawns!"

The tinted dawn had become an object in itself, like a waste-paper basket or the track for the dolly, a practical thing to have at hand and make use of. When all is said and done, these are the stories people who work in the cinema like to remember most, in fact they are the only ones they remember: the time there was a sudden downpour, the picnic was wrecked and people took shelter as best they could under a tree, inside the electricians' van, while the clever ones, like a benevolently presumptuous group of soldiers, made for a farmhouse and asked the peasants there to rustle up some omelettes.

This free and easy attitude, this casual interest, or, more appealingly, that playful air people in the film industry adopt towards people and things, as though the whole world were a film set at our disposal, or a huge props

A nostalgic shot from Amarcord, which is set in Fellini's native province of Romagna. "I am only partly romagnolo . . . But which side of me is the Romagna one? Keeping to the notion that the people of Romagna are extrovert, sensual, generous, very sociable, lovers of company, arguments and good food, passionately interested in politics, blasphemers who profess to be atheists but send their wives and daughters off to church because someone in the family at least must have links with the Almighty Father . . . I feel I display none of these such appealing virtues and shortcomings. When it comes to a passion for politics, I'm more of an Eskimo than a romagnolo."

department where we could lay our hands on what we liked without having to ask, is part of the alienation, the manipulation of the job. We are rather like painters for whom objects, faces, houses and sky are simply shapes they can depict as they wish. Through the cinema the whole world becomes an enormous still life, and even people's feelings are material that can be used. It is a frenzy, an intoxicating, near-divine thrill of great power, and this feeling, which speculators, raiders, plunderers and pioneers equally experience, creates the strongest bonds.

In the unit, you are all in the same boat for as long as the film takes; then you go your separate ways as though you had never known each other, like an army of mercenaries signed up by another prince, only to renew allegiance a year later with the same intensity. I like this part of it very much: it is the best form of socializing I have. The unit is a group which symbolizes society as a whole, but is all the more appealing because it comes together not to liberate slaves or feed the hungry, but to create an instrument of play, and this gives a special gentleness to the business of being together. The cinema offers you the illusion of being in the process of creating a world, a life. It is so enjoyable that you experience on a film set the same curiosity and sense of wonder that you have for life itself; and who would want to walk away from life? What is more, they pay you: to be paid for living is exhilarating. To leave a set for the last time where you have caused new human beings to exist, dress, speak and act is like being evicted from your own home.

On the last day of shooting *La dolce vita*, the final take was in the studio: a close-up of Anita Ekberg, sitting in Marcello Mastroianni's Triumph car with the wind in her hair. Her beauty was superhuman. The first time I saw her in a full-page photograph in an American magazine, I thought, ''My God, please don't let me meet her!'' Years later I was experiencing again that sense of rapt wonder, astonishment, disbelief which one feels at the sight of extraordinary creations such as the giraffe, the elephant or the baobab, when I saw her coming towards me, across the garden of the Hotel de la Ville, preceded, followed and flanked by three or four small men, her husband and her agents, who then

From Amarcord: *The Grand Hotel in Rimini as drawn by Fellini and (below) the concubines of an Arab Emir who are staying at the hotel. ''On summer evenings, the Grand Hotel would turn into Istanbul, Baghdad and Hollywood. On its terraces, screened off by plants with very thick foliage, Ziegfeld Follies style festivities may well have taken place: the seemingly golden bare backs of women encircled by arms of men in white dinner jackets; a perfumed breeze carrying snatches of syncopated musical trifles so sentimental as to make you swoon . . .''*

A set design for Amarcord *and (above) the end result recreating the Piazza delle Erbe in Rimini, the setting for the traditional ceremony of the "fogarazza," or bonfire, in which all the townspeople take part. On a spring night, they gather round with boxes, furniture and bundles of wood to build up the pyre with winter's left-overs; last of all, a* doll resembling an old woman is thrown on to the pyre, to the words, "Con sto fuoco, vecchietta mia/l'inverno e il gelo ti porti via" (With this flame, my old dame, today/take the winter cold far away); then the pyre is set alight. On pages 116–117: the astounding symbolical peacock of the Count of Lovignano, also from Amarcord.

vanished like shadows from around the halo of a source of light. It is my belief that Ekberg, above all, is incandescent.

She wanted to know about the script, whether the character was a forceful one, who the other actresses were, meanwhile drinking a large glass containing one of those multi-coloured cocktails with flags and straws, and speaking like a little girl with a cold, which made her all the more devastating. I seemed to be discovering the Platonic side of things, and in a state of total befuddlement I was murmuring to myself, ''Ah, so those are her ear lobes, those are her gums, this is the skin of a human being.'' That same evening I wanted to see Marcello Mastroianni, who listened to me through a haze of tobacco, looking a bit uneasy but trying to hide it: ''Get away with you! Really? You're not serious. All right, then,'' he said compliantly when I had finished my tale, raising his eyebrow the way Clark Gable used to, ''Let's have a look at her.''

Being a great connoisseur of men, Anita held out her hand to Marcello when he was introduced to her, but paid no attention to him, in fact she was already looking in a different direction, and throughout the evening she never said a word to him. Later Marcello, in the middle of something else, told me that Ekberg was not such a sensation after all. She reminded him very much of a German soldier in the Wehrmacht who had once tried to make him jump up on to a lorry during a round-up on Viale delle Milizie. Perhaps Marcello had felt offended, or ignored; that glorious, exquisite being, healthy as a shark, emanating the heat of a summer's day, instead of exhilarating him, had irritated him.

On that final day of *La dolce vita*, in a corner of the studio at Cinecittà, cluttered though it already was with bits of scenery for new films, a little party had been prepared to say goodbye to Anita. I went up to her and said to her: ''Well, Anita. It has been really wonderful. Now they all want to have a party in your honour. Leave your car here if you like, I'll have someone look after it, and then I'll take you along.'' ''No. No. No,'' she said. She gripped the steering wheel, and cried. She did not want to get out of the car. She did not want it all to be over.

Just before we started work on *Otto e mezzo* (8½), my mind suddenly went completely blank. I could not think what it was I wanted to do. Oh, I had made a whole lot of notes, I had even written down some dialogue and worked out the screenplay for it, the sets were being built. But the film . . . I no longer knew what was at the heart of it. One morning, no more than three or four days before we were due to start shooting, I sat down to type a letter to my producer, Rizzoli: "Dear Angelino, I am aware that what I am about to tell you will irreparably undermine our professional relationship. Our friendship will also be jeopardized by it. I ought to have written this letter to you three months ago, but up until last night I had hoped that . . ."

I was halfway through this letter when I heard my name being bawled by Menicuccio, the chief stage-hand, who was down in the courtyard below, asking me to pop over to the studio because Gasparino (another stage-hand) was celebrating his birthday and there was champagne all round, and he would be glad if I, "*il dottore*," could be there too.

So I went across to the studio. Carpenters, stage-hands and painters were all there waiting for me, glass in hand, on the set of the large kitchen which, give or take the odd distortion of memory, was meant to be the kitchen in my grandmother's house in the country. Gasparino, wearing a builder's cap and with a hammer dangling from his waist-belt, opened a bottle: "This is going to be a great film, *dottore*, here's to it! Long live *Otto e mezzo*!" He filled our glasses, everyone clapped, and I felt overcome with shame, I felt I was the lowest of the low, the captain abandoning his crew. I did not go back up to the office, where my letter of escape

T̶wo stills from Il Casanova
di Federico Fellini *(Fellini's
Casanova, 1976), freely adapted
from* Storia della mia vita *(Story
of my life) by the eighteenth-
century Venetian libertine
Giacomo Casanova. "I see
Casanova's sexual love as
obsessive, the shocking, mechanical
eros of a human piston. It is the*

*Catholic eros of those who see
females as animals or angels, never
as women, and who only
experience sexual intercourse as a
means to finding themselves . . .
Casanova never existed as an
individual: he only imagined that
he existed. He was alive only in the
projections of himself which he
created . . ."*

was waiting for me half finished, but went and sat on a bench in the garden, in the midst of all the busy comings and goings of workmen, technicians and actors attached to the other film companies at work there. I felt empty, blank. I realized that I was in a difficult position and there was no getting out of it. I was a director who wanted to make a film he could no longer remember. And suddenly, in that very moment I found myself at the heart of the film – I would tell the story of everything that was happening to me, I would make a film about the story of a director who no longer knows what kind of film it is he wants to make.

Studio 5 has been the most important setting for me in Cinecittà. I have worked there more than in the other studios: it is the biggest film studio in the world, they say. I do not know about that, but the studios at Paramount which I saw in Los Angeles are certainly very small by comparison. In Studio 5, in August 1959, the set designer Pietro Gherardi completely reconstructed Rome's Via Veneto for *La dolce vita*; and from that moment on, for me Cinecittà has become a substitute for the world.

There were practical reasons of organization which made it necessary to reconstruct Via Veneto. In fact, when shooting began on *La dolce vita*, Via Veneto itself became the problem. The city authorities only allowed filming to take place in this street between two and six o'clock in the morning, and the permit had a lot of conditions attached. For the scene in which Marcello Mastroianni takes Anita back home after her revel in the Trevi Fountain, there were no difficulties. We waited for the dead of night and managed to get a really beautiful dawn, Anita with her teeth chattering from the cold, and Marcello worried about the punches he was supposed to take from the athletic Lex Barker, and the paparazzi dancing around the set like little demons. But the scene in the car between Marcello and Anouk Aimée, for which I did not want to use back projection, was more complicated. There were endless negotiations with the traffic police and in the end we obtained the permit to shoot the scene driving along, provided we did not stop once, because that would hold up the traffic. A motorcade was organized which looked like the procession of the Magi. I

VENUSIA

From Il Casanova di Federico Fellini, *left: a drawing by Fellini for the great effigy of the woman's head, a symbol of Venice, which in the Venetian festivities at the beginning of the film is pulled up out of Grand Canal and immediately sinks again. Below: the scene as it is in the film. Right: the remains of the woman's head left out in the grounds at Cinecittà. Even Venice itself was rebuilt in the studio, with the Cinecittà swimming-pool used to suggest the lagoon and the canals. "I needed a Venice which had more water, water everywhere, a city like a confining amniotic sac, or a full bladder."*

was in front in my car, half turned round to see what was happening behind. Marcello and Anouk were following, in the open top Cadillac. Anouk hardly knew how to drive, but the scene required her to be at the wheel: she was pale, tense, and her heart pounded. Next to her Mastroianni, who prided himself on being an experienced driver, suffered indescribably. Behind them came the camera car with the camera mounted on it, and then the horde of cars with the production team, while at the sides of the long column the Fiat 600s and scooters of the assistants moved at speed.

As the scene had to be re-taken several times, we went over the route again and again, round the block and forming the column up again in Via Ludovisi. A number of people had gathered along the pavements to watch this procession go by, horns blaring and rather a ham affair, as cinema invariably is when it happens in public. I particularly remember the face of one onlooker in front of the Excelsior, a bloke with a little beret, and a face as dark-skinned as a Saracen. He waited eagerly each time round for me to come past, and knowing full well that I could not stop without bringing about the end of the world, would bide his time until I was three or four feet from his face, and would then shout an absolutely unrepeatable oath at me in Roman dialect. This happened four, five, six times: the minute I reached the traffic lights, this Saracen eyed me from a distance with a sneer, looking forward to the pleasure of insulting me again. Then, as I drew level with him, bang, every time he unleashed this word, always the same one, but uttered with a crescendo of enthusiasm. On the seventh circuit I was at the end of my tether, and would have stopped filming so that I could get out and grab hold of him by the scruff of his neck, had I not been afraid that such an action might well compromise an entire night's work. I confined myself to telling him where he could get off, using indecorous expressions and gestures which could only be justified by the impotent rage of that moment. As soon as shooting was over, and the procession had disbanded in Via

T wo dance scenes from Il Casanova di Federico Fellini. Right: a dance that takes place, during a party, between the rich homosexual patron Du Bois dressed as a mantis, and his lover as a male mantis in the made-up short opera "The Praying Mantis." Opposite: Casanova (played by Donald Sutherland) remembering the last time he danced in Venice, with the only woman he could, Rosalba the mechanical doll (the actress Adele Angela Lojodice).

Sardegna, I asked a couple of the burliest stage-hands to come with me and ran in the direction of the Excelsior to sort him out. But my vituperative friend had gone, vanished into thin air. To this day I have the image of him imprinted on my memory, little beret, the lot, and I have not given up hope that I shall meet him one of these days.

It was the shock of this episode which made me persuade the production side that we should reconstruct Via Veneto. I had to shoot several scenes around pavement coffee tables, including the scene where Marcello meets his father, and it was absolutely out of the question to try and work late at night or shooting from a hidden camera. The reconstruction of Via Veneto by Gherardi at Cinecittà was exact down to the very last detail, but it had a distinctive feature: it was on the flat instead of uphill. From working on the set and becoming so familiar with those surroundings, my dislike of the real Via Veneto grew even more, so much that I imagine I will never be rid of it. When I go past the Café de Paris, I cannot stop myself thinking that the authentic Via Veneto was the one in Studio 5, and that the dimensions of the street in the studio were more accurate or certainly more attractive. I also get an overwhelming desire to exercise the same tyrannical authority, which I had over the make-believe one, over the street in real life. Reconstructing everything in the studio has, with the passing of time, become something I increasingly cannot do without, so much so that it always surprises me when people ask me why I do it.

I film in the studio in order to capture a subjective reality which has been purified of those incidental aspects of real life which are of no use to me. Photography captures everything it sees. On the other hand, a process which is geared to making the film camera photograph a feeling, a premonition, a yearning, needs a selective reality devoid of irrelevant details which would distract or overload it. Your memory of things and places automatically carries out this selective function, filtering the mental pictures, eliminating superfluous elements, and focusing on the essence of the feeling. The portraying of life through film therefore needs a space which is similar to that of your imaginative world. Let me give you an example. When as adults we go back to visit the places we grew up in, they seem to us to be smaller than we remember. If you want to portray this impression, the astonishment and sense of the unreal, you have to recreate the magnified dimensions which in childhood occur naturally. So you need a space to illuminate, darken, magnify and reduce; a space in which to bring together those features you associate with a place so it is immediately recognizable, and at the same time reproduces a feeling.

Theater sets have always been very much a part of my film-making; when I was a child, puppet theaters were the toy I most wanted and was given. From an early age I always messed about with scissors, paints, brushes, modelling clay, glue, chalk and papier-mâché, and played with great meccano sets, and play-kits such as "The Little Carpenter" and "The Little Engineer."

Theater scenery and the illusions they create, have been a constant fascination to me. When I was young, we used to live in a house near the railway station in Rimini. It was a small town house with a front garden. The big garden at the back led to an enormous building (it could have been a barracks or a church) on which someone had written in white letters in a semicircle: "Poli . . . ma riminese." Two letters from the first word had dropped off and been lost.

As our garden was sunken, the ground on which this building stood, on the other side of the garden wall, seemed higher, right up high. One morning I was in the garden making a bow out of a stick, when all of a sudden there was a deafening noise. It was the formidable sound of the theater's shutter, which I had never noticed before and was now being rolled up, eventually revealing a huge black entrance. In the middle of this entrance were a man wearing a little beret and a raincoat and a woman who was knitting. The dialogue between them went like this. Man: "The murderer must have got in through the window." Woman: "The window is shut." Man: "Sergeant Jonathan has found signs of a break-in." Then the man turned towards where I was standing in the garden. "Are there any figs on that tree?" "I don't know."

They were rehearsing the Grand Guignol; it was Bella Starace Sainati's company. The man lifted me up and into the dark cavern. I saw gold-coloured platforms, and, right beside me, the underbelly of a locomotive which was hanging from ropes and swaying in midair, against a background of red, white and yellow celluloid. This was the theater. The man went on talking about the problem of the window. I did not understand if it was a game or what. A long time might well have passed, and then suddenly I heard my mother's voice calling me in. "The soup is on the table." The man with

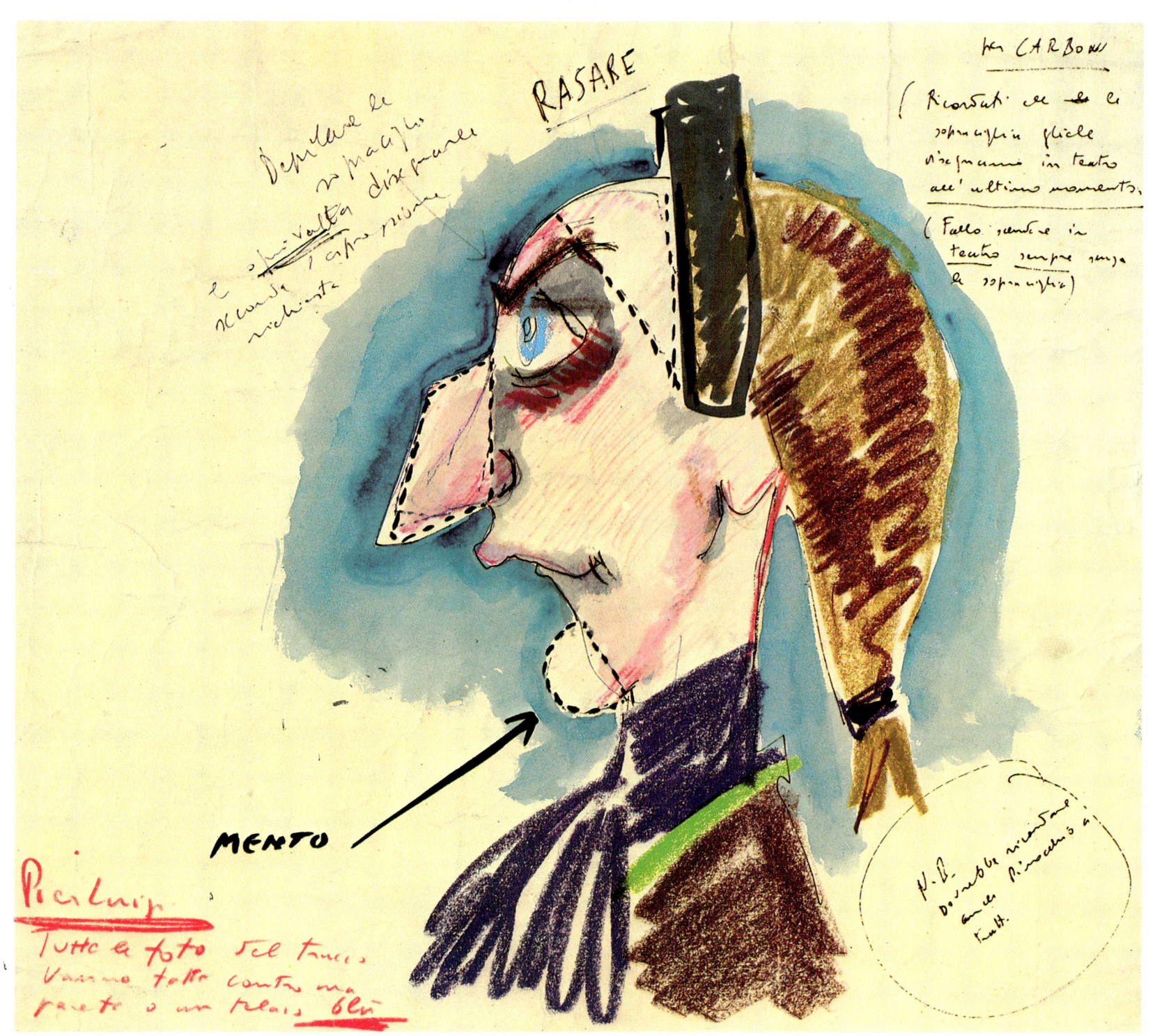

A drawing by Fellini for the character of Casanova from Il Casanova di Federico Fellini, with instructions to the set photographer and the make-up artist, and a general note: "He ought to look like Pinocchio as well." During shooting on the film, Casanova had forty costume changes, ten wigs, three hundred noses, and another three hundred chins, amounting to one hundred and twenty-six make-up changes in all. "Sutherland, who is shorter than the real Casanova (who was over six feet three inches tall) has an ideal face for the part: absent features, a hazy, watery look, with something shapeless about it, like a jelly-fish, which makes it easier to re-mould."

the little beret helped me back over the wall. Two evenings later, my parents took me to see the play. My mother tells how I stayed stock still throughout the performance. The locomotive emerged from the darkness of the night and was about to run over a woman tied to the track, and then the woman was saved just as an enormous, heavy, soft red curtain came down, narrowly missing her. The excitement of it lasted all night.

But what happens when, as with *Satyricon*, you find yourself confronted by sets you have no idea about, a theatrical enigma, an unknown world for which you have neither memories nor feelings? The reason why Petronius's *Satyricon* is such a mysterious text is because it is fragmentary. And yet this fragmentation is in some way symbolic. Symbolic of the general fragmented nature of the ancient world as it appears to us now. This is the real fascination of the text and of the world portrayed inside it. For the film, I found myself contemplating an unknown landscape, enveloped in a thick mist which lifted in places and revealed the world it hid; the world of antiquity is for me a lost world, one with which my ignorance prevents me from having more than a fantastic, imaginative relationship fed by theories and possibilities which have no connection with historical fact or knowledge.

Where could I start? What did I have to reconstruct at Cinecittà? The ruins of Ancient Rome? The Appian Way? Or rather those photographs of Roman ruins and the Appian Way you see in history books or on postcards? Plausible ghosts, bloodless images, graveyard perspectives heavy with funereal gloom for the delightful pictures of those photographers, in particular the Germans, who portray these ruins at sunset, in a dim light, and with a couple of little sheep in the foreground. The frescoes of Pompeii, perhaps? Or Herculaneum? The exhibits at the Capitoline Museum, deadened as they are by their awful scholastic presentation, had left me unmoved. The incredible inertia of the finds which fill the Museum means they can only offer you the familiar picture created by the ideas of teachers or the chance stimulation of personal associations. At one

Three scenes from Il Casanova di Federico Fellini *showing the studio and swimming-pool set for "Annamaria's house" in Venice. Opposite: Fellini's sketch and, top, the house as it appears in the film. Below: the scene being* filmed at Cinecittà. "The women Casanova sees in his memory all have coral lips, teeth like pearls, alabaster cheeks, wasp waists and hair as black as a raven's wing. Of the two to three hundred women Casanova talks about, there's not one he manages to remember as she really was; it's quite something if he can recall one of their names . . ." On pages 130–131: the scene of the performance of "Orpheus and Eurydice" at the Dresden Theater, also from the film.

point I thought I recognized a bust in marble with empty eyes. It had the thin, startled little face of a country cousin of mine – her name was Jole, and she had red hair; whenever I saw her, she was ill in bed, and had to drink all the time. For a split second I had the impression that an invisible link had been established, some sort of elusive complicity between us; that bust had Jole's face, and I stroked her curly stone hair. "Perhaps you can help me a little . . . Solonina?" (There was a small plaque round her neck with this name written on it); but just as I was having these thoughts, the learned friend who was with me told me that Solonina's speciality was massacres and crucifixions, and that her greatest pleasure in life was to tear her victims' hearts out with her bare hands during human sacrificial rites.

The choice of faces for *Satyricon* also left me lost and confused. In general, the human element in a film of mine is the surest means, the most accurate path to follow to find the

real meaning; but this time there were no models, no aesthetic norms to abide by, or at any rate none that tallied with what it was I vaguely felt I wanted to do. All the conventional forms of expression were upset, turned upside down, and if I had let myself try and use them, the result could have been unforeseeably disastrous. If I happened to remark: "Aha, now that one has the face of a Roman," once in costume and make-up the same actor would look more like a clerk or a tram driver. When you look at the head of Messalina, it has the placid, chubby features of a woman selling eggs.

Perhaps one night, at the Colosseum . . . that horrific moon-shaped catastrophe in stone, that huge skull eaten away by time, stranded in the middle of the city, had appeared to me for a split second as a relic of the civilization of another planet and sent a shiver of terror and delight through me. A split second; but for the first time I had felt immersed in the swirling clarity of dreams and the feverish hot-house of premonition and fantasy.

I ended up by creating a Roman world as evoked by a spiritual, out-of-the-body experience, based on the ideas, doubts and questions I had jotted down in my director's notebook.

I DON'T KNOW YOU.

WHO ARE YOU?

NAZIS – RACISTS – YODELS

MINERAL – NEUROTIC – HALLUCINATING – PSYCHEDELIC

BARBARIC – SCIENCE-FICTIONAL

MARTIANS – MADHOUSE

There is a different edge to the atmosphere. Do you remember the dream of the fat people, pink, dazed, in the cells of the madhouse?

Fibrillation. OVERHEATED.

LA CITTÀ DELLE DONNE

How to attempt to reconstruct a very early amphora, using shards found centuries later.

Dust – Darkness (Evocation)

Finish eventually with more bits missing, broken; fragments . . . ". . . the old man laughed, pointing at something in the echo . . ."

". . . the horse dripping with sweat . . ."

". . . his eyes had taken on a melancholy look."

DARKNESS – BLACK TAILS – RAUCOUS VOICES THAT GURGLE INCREASINGLY TORTUOUS PHRASES. DROWNED PEOPLE WHO ARE TRYING TO SPEAK.

REMEMBER:

The shocking fixity of bas-reliefs. Empty eyes. No pupils. Eyes of bronze.

The holidays – The night was all studded with fires of joy. Many houses being built. Bridges. Collapses. (Earthquake on Insula Felix, the terrifying great skyscraper block, huge, dark, swarming like Brueghel's Tower of Babel.)

A film about the Martians. It should create the same fascination with suspense and tension which the earliest Japanese films had for us: you never knew if those characters were laughing or crying, the sudden leaps, the brutish yells of Toshiro Mifune used to make your heart miss a beat: would he put his arms round you like a brother or split you in two with one blow of his scimitar?

UNRHYTHMICAL – SKINNY – OBLIQUE – UNFORESEEABLE

Exasperating slowness, the speed of microbes.

BADLY PERFORMED, with very long silences, speech impediments. Broken, hesitant; an impersonal dubbing track, ascetic, like news readers on radio. A technically inaccurate dub, with voices ending before the lips stop moving, or going on after they have stopped; enough to horrify the sound technicians, and especially the Americans who, when shown a shot pulsating with hundreds of sailors mutinying and berserk in a storm at sea, take great pains to watch avidly whether the commands given by the admiral coincide with his lip movements.

Drawings by Fellini for Roma *and* La città delle donne *(The City of Women). "Sketchers, caricaturists, painters, even those artists who draw the Virgin Mary in chalks on the pavement, always fascinated me. They fill me with awe, almost as much as actors used to. I say actors, but I really mean actresses. I have always enjoyed browsing through the studios of painters, in their garrets, and spending whole afternoons in those large draughty and untidy rooms where sculptors work, feeling totally at home . . ."*

A great fable, beguiling and mysterious. A film of still shots, completely static; no tracking shots, no other camera movements. A film to be simply contemplated, just like a dream; and you end up hypnotized by it. Everything will be unconnected and fragmentary. And yet at the same time strangely homogeneous. Every detail will stand on its own merits, isolated, magnified, absurd, monstrous, just as in dreams. A lot of dark, a lot of night, a lot of shadowy settings, dimly lit. Or landscapes similar to limbo, bathed in unreal, washed out, dream-like sunshine. Many corridors, ambulatories, rooms, courtyards, alleyways, stairways and other similar narrow distressing passages. Nothing luminous, white, shining. Clothes all dirty opaque colours, suggestive of stone, dust, mud. Colours like black, yellow, red, but all of them smothered by a continual shower of ashes. In a figurative sense, I will try to effect a hybrid of Pompeii and psychedelia, Byzantine art and pop art, Mondrian and Klee with barbarian art . . . a magmatic freeing of images.

REMEMBER:

DISJOINTED PROPORTIONS.

LITTLE MEN IN THE FOREGROUND AND GIANTS IN THE BACKGROUND.

The Colossus of Nero transported on a cart through the alleys of the Subura slums.

MAKE-UP for the *animals* (I want to do this myself!)

UNKNOWN ANIMALS FROM EXTINCT SPECIES

IMPORTANT: gestures, winks, grimaces which allude to understandings that cannot be decoded. Fixed looks. Or wandering, feverishly (and if GITON were to express himself only through sign language, miming things, people, events in a fascinating, sibylline algebra of his own, like Harpo Marx?)

LUPERCALIA.

The statues of Venus and Mars with loadstones in their navels, are powerfully attracted to each other. . . . out loud: "The night is over. The night is over."

Production shots from La città delle donne *(1980), the film about women who changed during the years of feminism and those who remained ingrained in the old mould. Among the trees in the pine forest at Fregene, Fellini shows actress Berenice Stegers how to kiss Marcello Mastroianni when she meets him off the train. "Since I was a boy, I've liked warm women who inspire confidence, the ones who are full-bodied and as soft as a wet nurse, brunettes with large mouths, smiling and sensual women, women who make you uneasy, blonde women who are cruel, serious and distant, a bit sadistic . . . I have never really grown out of the erotic tastes of adolescence."*

*F*ellini the director at work, shooting a scene from La città delle donne *and in a cartoon self-portrait. In the dream-like expansiveness of the film, everything takes on abnormal proportions: an equestrian monument to Queen Christina of Sweden, the archetypal cultured and powerful woman, becomes twenty feet high, a guard-dog is more than six feet tall, a beautiful white-skinned bottom stands sixty feet high, and the welcoming, redeeming woman who comes in a fire-balloon to rescue the hero from his nightmare is simply massive, vast. Opposite: the high boxing ring, right under the ceiling, with the tragic air of a pagan altar where human sacrifices are offered up, in which a number of gladiators take on the ideal woman watched by an all-female crowd.*

The basic tool in the film director's expression kit is lighting. It is inconceivable and inadmissible that anyone wanting to express himself through images should not accept that light is as much his concern as the plot of the film. The cinema is image, and light is the most crucial element of image. I never get tired of saying this: light is the ideology of cinema; it is feeling, colour, tone, depth, atmosphere and narrative. Light is a miracle worker, adding, blotting out, reducing, enriching, shading, emphasizing, hinting, making the fantastic and the substance of dreams appear credible and acceptable, or, on the contrary, adding quivering transparent effects and making an illusion out of the greyest everyday reality. With a floodlight and a couple of panels, an opaque, inexpressive face becomes intelligent, mysterious and fascinating; a kindly, warm face can turn sinister, threatening, and cruel. The most basic and crudely executed set design can, with the effective use of lighting, reveal surprising

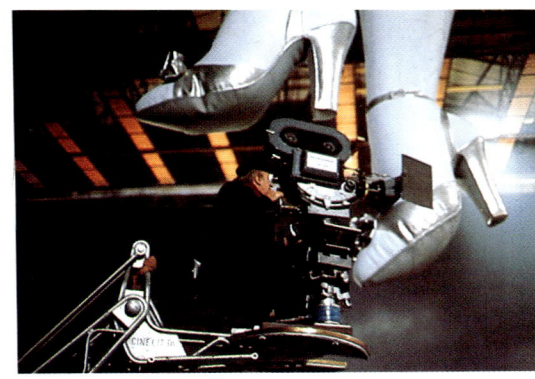

perspectives and bring the story to life in a suspenseful atmosphere which is tense and disturbing; or, by moving one strong lamp, and bringing up another as back lighting, lo and behold all hint of stress vanishes and everything becomes calm and homely once more. A film should be written through light, and style expressed through light. This is why you need to have an empty space to furnish with feeling and memory, and total control over light. So a film studio has become for me the only place where expression is possible. Studio 5 at Cinecittà is the ideal setting. Utter excitement, thrill, ecstasy, is what I experience when confronted by an empty studio, a space to be filled, and a world to be created.

All encounters, relationships, friendships, experiences and journeys begin and end for me in the studios of Cinecittà: everything that exists outside the gates of Cinecittà can be seen as a vast deposit box to be visited, raided, and brought eagerly and tirelessly into Cinecittà. Perhaps it is a privilege, perhaps a form of enslavement, but it is my way of being. As is my wont, when I set my film *Intervista* at Cinecittà, I actually reconstructed Cinecittà itself there too, like every other reality I have created. The Cinecittà which appears to be seen from the air at the beginning of the film was a mock-up. I could have done aerial shots from a helicopter, but the result would have looked more like a map of the place, which because it is real does not mean anything, does not communicate any particular feeling. No, I wanted to do Cinecittà differently: using the model, I was able to re-route the avenues of pine trees, give the tarred roofs a different colour, and by making the buildings all grey, give them a kind of official format without any real sculptural quality.

Trick shots, special effects . . . It can sometimes happen that no matter what the prognostication, the lighting does not manage to give the necessary allusive aura to some sets. You do not succeed in setting the scene in the past to depict a memory and removing the feel of the present. When that is the case, all you need is a veil of invisible mist, rather like a painter's glaze, to cream off the excess of substantiality and solidity and lend an added sense of remoteness. It is the same with sound. When work on the mixing of each film

Photographs taken during the filming of La città delle donne *at Cinecittà showing the hero being made to climb into the air balloon's basket by an old woman. The balloon is shaped like a voluptuous young woman, her head encircled by a halo of electric light-bulbs. The hero, aloft in the starry sky in the balloon basket, experiences a moment of magical happiness; but in the closing scene of the film, a burst of machine-gun fire from a woman terrorist on the ground below punctures the balloon and brings the basket crashing down.*

starts, I go to the microphone and produce a whole series of sighs, a breathing sound which is recorded by the technicians on what they call "Dr Fellini's airwaves." When the words of the film's dialogue sound as though they are falling in space, this imperceptible breathing, used as an aural underlay, eliminates the empty echo of the room and animates the sound with something which is not, itself, clearly identifiable.

As happens in school or in love, the shooting of a film begins to finish a little before the end. A film has so many ways of taking its leave of its author: at Cinecittà, a set is dismantled, an actor goes away, the unit dwindles . . . "Can I say goodbye to you now, *dottore*? I'm starting a new film tomorrow." The last two weeks of filming are the time when these goodbyes come thick and fast, the happiness in them reminiscent of schoolchildren breaking up for the summer. Even though cinema people, either through interest or

vocation, usually do their job very willingly (needless to say, the director would like them all to be even more enthusiastic, involved and happy), the work always has something to do with obligation and close cooperation. Because of this, the gradual disbanding of the company, the sense that the film is in its final week, communicates a certain carefree light-heartedness. It is different for the director: he has already begun to guide his film into another phase, the editing of it. For a director like me, who makes films to provide translations of life itself, the end of a film is just like its beginning – just as the end or beginning of the academic year is for a teacher who has been teaching for fifty years— and it is a moment he is all too familiar with.

Nobody gets particularly sad about it. All of a sudden, one morning, everything seems as before. As always, I have waited for the production car in front of the Café Canova in Piazza del Popolo, as usual I have sat in front next to the

*F*rom La città delle donne, shots of the roller coaster, a chute festooned with multi-coloured lights which travels up and down at great speed. The hero gets on to it through a tunnel and while on it relives the traumatic experience of his sexual initiation; during the trip he confronts again, though now they are magnified or distorted by the shifting perspectives of memory, the disturbances, enchantments and terrors of his earliest encounters with the female form. The hero is dressed like a child of the past in a long white nightshirt, and resembles Little Nemo, the infant dreamer character in the American cartoons by Winsor McCay from the beginning of the century.

driver, and we have driven to Cinecittà. But on arrival, you realize from the way the guards wave to you and from the fact that the workmen are lying in the sun, that today is the last day. All those who used to crowd round you to say hello are either not there any longer, or the way they greet you makes you feel you are at the window of a train about to leave. The secretaries are all in a different mood now. Along the corridor of my office-apartment, there is no longer the frenzied activity of a hotel kitchen, and the cook is not making triumphant announcements about the interests of her guests, like: "I've got some very nice mullet for today, *dottore*." Everything has changed.

So you no longer go into the studio but to the editing suite. The job is not done in a big building like an aircraft hangar, but in a separate block along Cinecittà's tree-lined avenues. You climb a staircase where you encounter no Abyssinians, astronauts or odalisques, but people in black or white shirts. In the studio I never get tired, I can even work for thirty hours at a stretch, because I find that circus atmosphere so congenial, it recharges my batteries; at the editing table I cannot work for more than two hours, two and a half at the most; editing gives you the kind of tension a pilot feels at the moment of touch-down. In the studio, nothing troubles me, whether it is schoolchildren visiting, friends, journalists, Japanese visitors with their little cameras, ambassadors, or noise; the floodlight isolates me, makes me feel like I am in a spacesuit. In the editing suite, on the other hand, I cannot have people there or endure being disturbed. It is the moment when Frankenstein looks at the Creature he has created, watches for the Monster to open his eyes, breathe, move. In the studio I am always in good health. Sometimes I have turned up there running a temperature. But once I have said hello to the camera operator and my friends, the lights are on, and I am seated on the dolly being propelled along by the workmen like a Chinese Emperor, the temperature has gone. In this way, when you are working from the heart and fulfilling the truest part of yourself, you are actually as well as you can be. When I am editing, though, I find things annoying, irritating and intolerable.

When you go into the editing suite, the assistants make a fuss of you, and say things like "Are you all right?" or "We've had an outside line laid on for you, so you can make all the calls you like from here," and the editor greeting you points to the round cans containing the film in piles which almost reach the ceiling, as though to say, "You certainly unburdened yourself in this one, didn't you?"

But as the years have passed, I have gone on reducing the number of takes, I shoot less each time. Ninety per cent of the scenes in *Intervista* were shot with a single take, first time. Time has instilled in me the belief that if you have rehearsed properly, the first take is the best; because the first take is the big plunge, when you say "action," you are releasing a flow, a tension, an act of giving birth which cannot recapture the same degree of spontaneity and inspiration if it has to be done again. I cannot understand those of my fellow directors who will go to thirty-five, sixty, even seventy takes; perhaps they are spurred on by the absurd hope that by trying again and again, the shot can miraculously improve, and perhaps they experience some kind of intoxicating sense of power when they see that these thirty or one hundred people in the company will follow the director's instructions yet again, until the director says he is happy with it. In the past, I have done more takes too, but seeing the clapper board operator rubbing out one take number and writing in the next over and over again, I feel embarrassed, and I do not think I have ever gone beyond Take Ten, not since I started. But with the years, the impatience which is part of my make-up has become more demanding, and I have a sharper recollection of the irony of the directors in the old days who used to say: "Well, you can only use one version at the end of the day."

I feel I am on their side, closer to an approach which will play down the whole process, as opposed to a mystique of rigid, implacable discipline. The work done by someone who claims to produce shadows, shapes, perspectives and lights at the drop of a hat involves a combination of discipline and flexibility. You have to be intransigent and implacable, but also flexible, careful to pick up on resistance, incompatibilities, and possible errors, in a spirit of

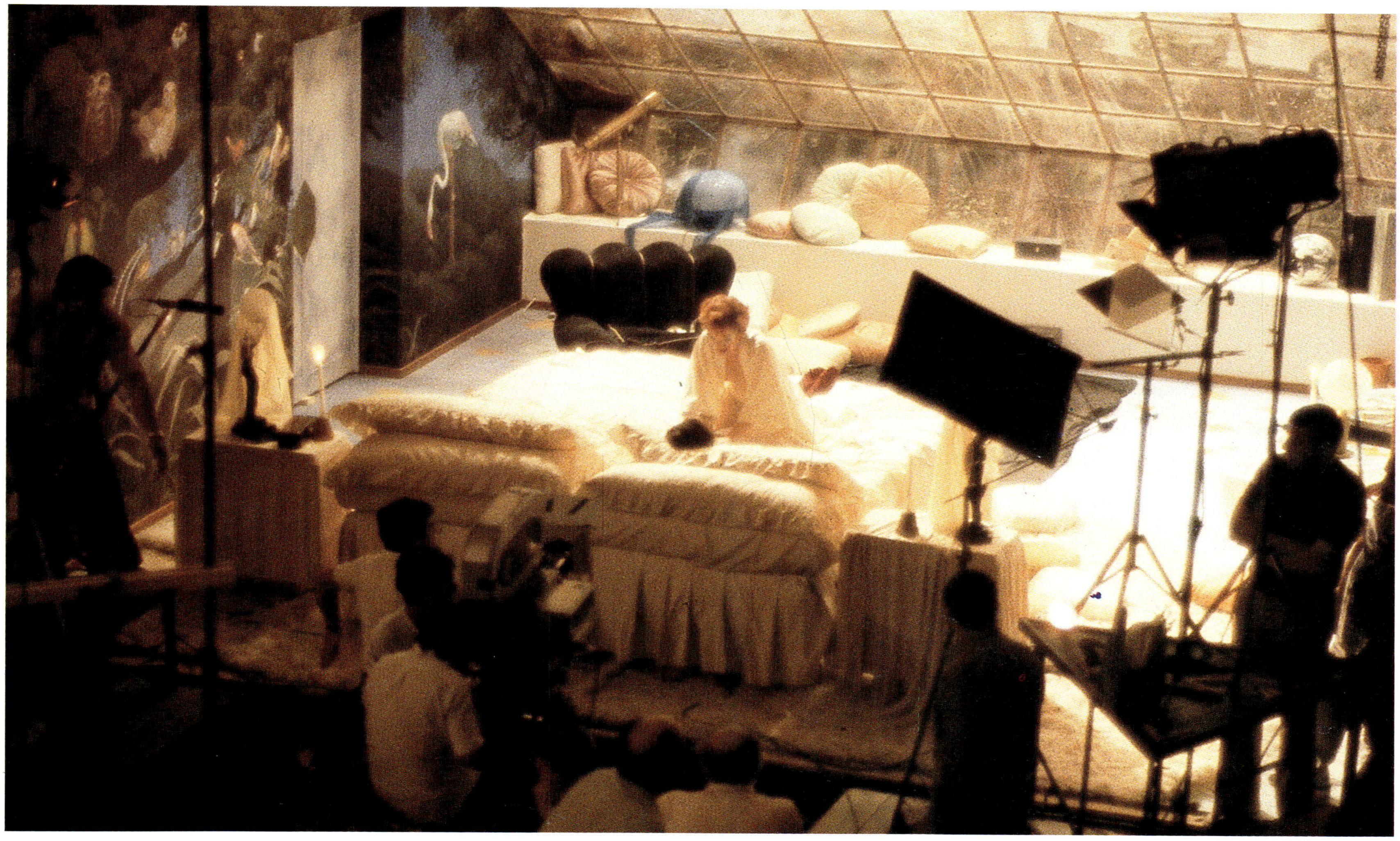

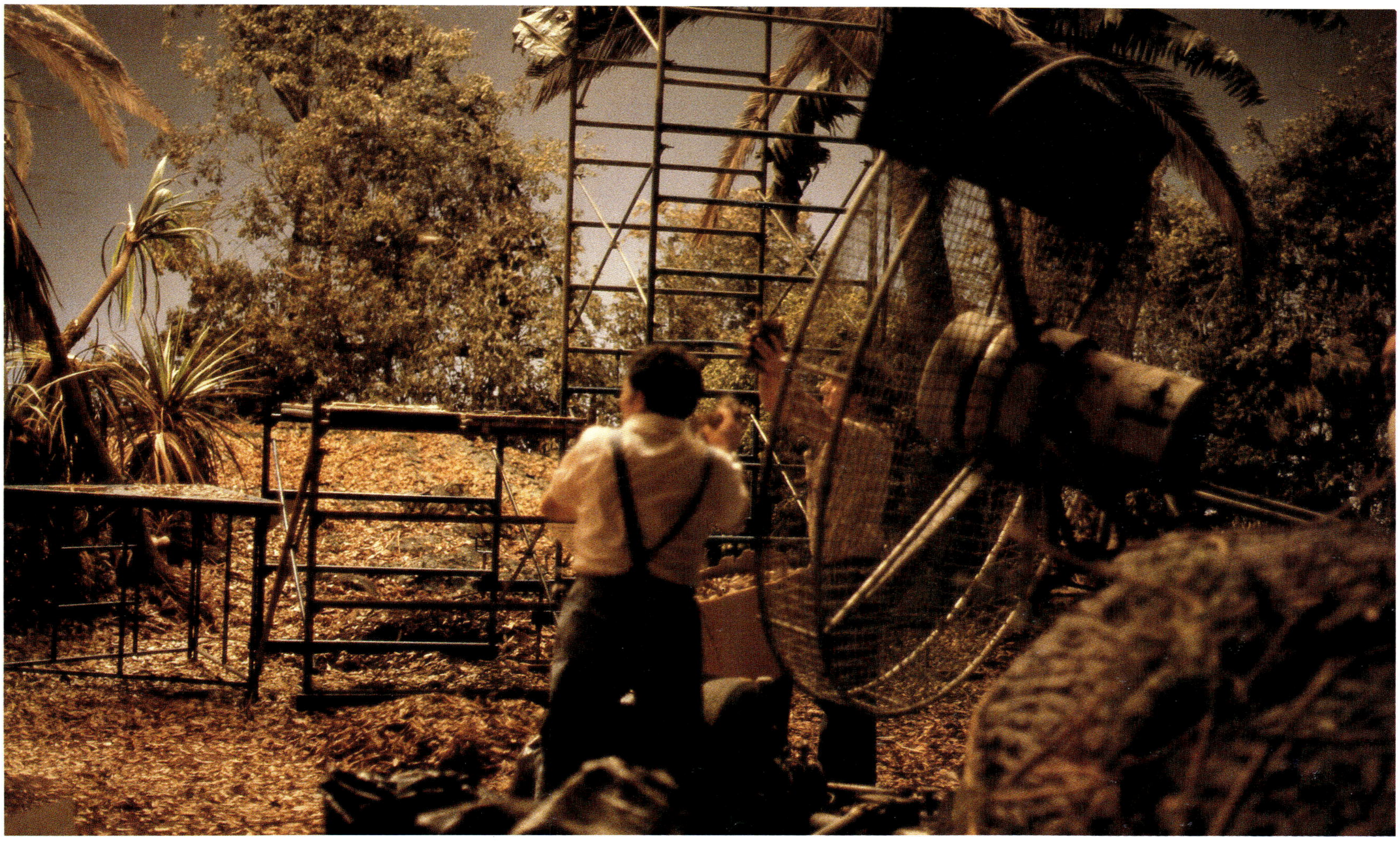

vigilant responsibility. The unforeseen element is by no means always exclusively a difficulty; it can often be a help, and everything that happens after you have an idea for a particular film and during its preparation, filming, and editing, will be of use to the film. Everything is part of the film: an actor's illness which means that he has to be replaced, the artful stubbornness of a producer, or an accident which holds up shooting. These are not obstacles but the very elements of which the film is gradually being composed. What occurs always ends up by having the upper hand, taking the place of what could have been or ought to have been. The unforeseen things are not just part of the journey, but the journey itself. It is essential to retain a clear inner receptiveness. Making a film does not mean obstinately trying to adapt reality to preconceived ideas. Making a film also involves being able to recognize, accept and make use of the gradual changes to your original ideas brought about by what is at the same time happening alongside them. You have to have absolute faith in what you are doing, of course, but also the ability to accept what is being revealed as the process unfolds, because often this *is* what you want to do, only you have been constantly suppressing it up till then. This means accepting the fact that even if you have renounced many things and you feel that you have not achieved the illusion you hoped for or the image is not satisfyingly rarefied any more, what you *have* done is fine anyway, for the simple reason that it *is* what has been done. Usually I work on the editing for a couple of months. Often you hear somebody unqualified claim that the film is created at the editing stage. That has never happened to me. A film-maker decides on the editing while he is shooting the film. Constructing a film is like constructing a living work; the imaginative structure of the film is ever present and unchangeable in all its stages, and no director, however reckless and unscrupulous, can allow himself to take out the vital parts of the story he is telling and bring them in later instead.

Editing reasserts the breath and the rhythm of the film which you should already have created and established

*F*ellini's sketch (far left) for one of the ships in E la nave va (And the Ship Sails On, *1983); the model of the steamer* Gloria N. *on which the main characters in the film are passengers, and (below) the vessel out at sea in a scene from the film.*

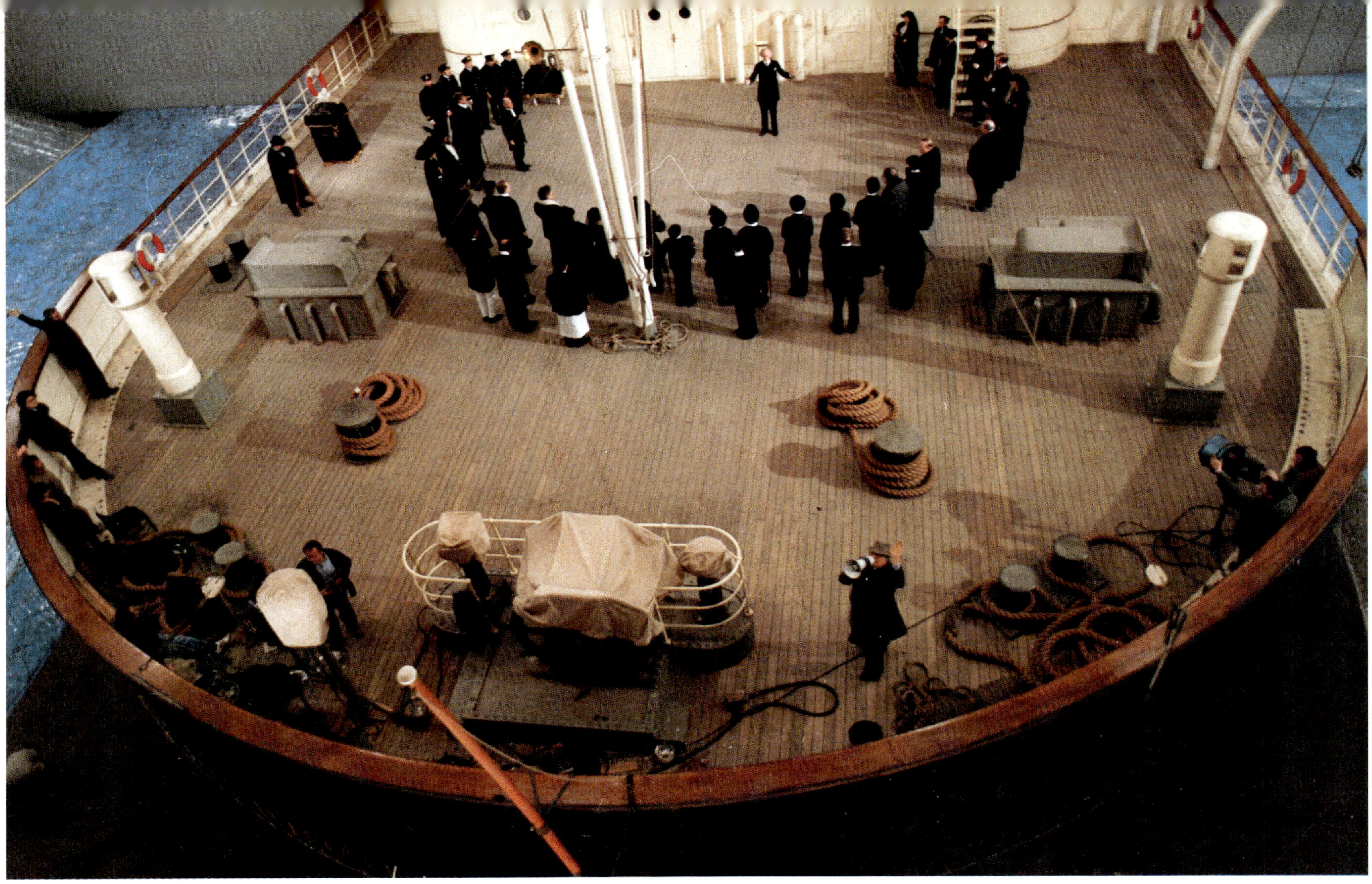

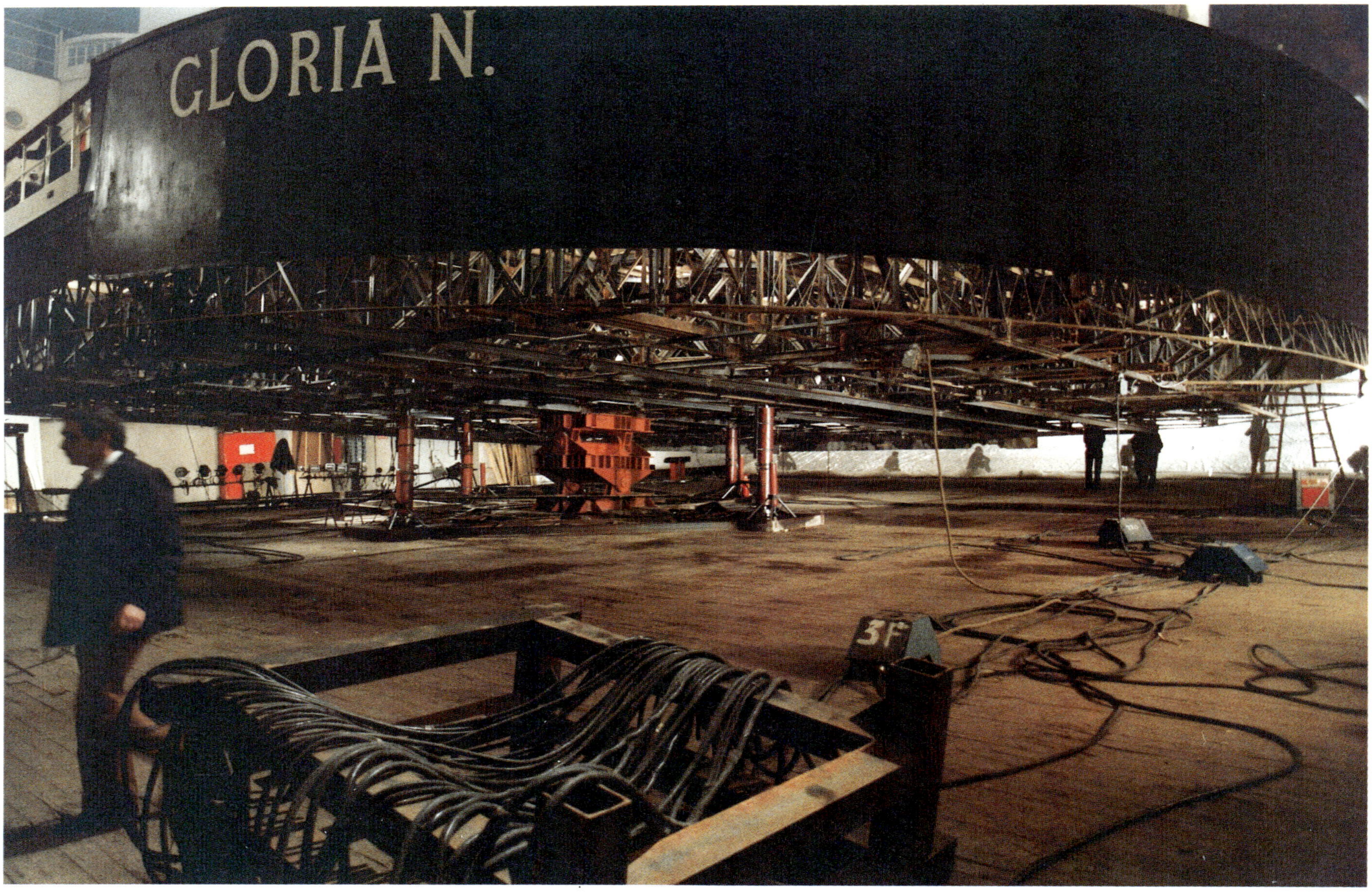
GLORIA N.
3F

at the shooting stage. During editing, you can choose to up or down the tempo of someone breathing, if you think that is called for, or interrupt the length and fixity of an image.

Then the film is transferred from the small screen of the movieola where it had begun to be familiar and friendly, and returns to fill the cinema-sized screen for the later stages of editing. Is it still your film? Do you still recognize it?

All the subsequent phases transform it, change it further, so that every time you see it, it is different. One moment it is youthful, and very happy, the next it is hobbling, full of aches and pains, suffering from old age; it can be quick, swift and lissom, or limping, slow, and paralyzed. The images are its own, the ones it has managed to win for itself, and the ones with which I have tried to keep up with it. Surrounding these images is the noise of the guide track, as well as the ragbag of sound from daily life on the set, shouts, imprecations, laughter, or silences which were hard to achieve. A kind of umbilical cord still keeps us attached to the film. What no longer exists between us and the film (at this point it becomes an object, while for someone else maybe it is now that it comes to life) is the friendship we fought for previously or the difficult feeling of solidarity.

Before I start dubbing, I have the film screened without the production soundtrack, in a completely silent version. I have to be on my own when I watch it then, because I need to see whether over and above the story I wanted to tell, the dream language of the film is sufficient in itself. Whether this silence, which has the effect of putting back into cinema the spellbinding fascination of its historical muteness, makes the images I have made into likenesses of those voiceless fantasies which had first come to me in the flashing darkness of the imagination, like a magic "Coming Shortly" whose job it was to convey the idea of the film as a whole.

The Cinefonico, a small block at Cinecittà on the avenue resounding non-stop with music, gunfire, battle sounds and voices, is the venue for the next stage, the dubbing. This is one of my hardest tasks. I have never been able to shoot a

In E la nave va *the* Gloria N. *never left Studio 5 at Cinecittà. "We made this authentic period steamer right there, complete with engine room, cabins, saloons and every last detail meticulously reconstructed after studying hundreds of plans and photographs with the architect Dante Ferretti. In order to suggest the vessel's mobility and its continual rolling motion on the waves, we mounted it on a complicated balancing scale which was activated and regulated by means of a computer simulating the movement of a ship out at sea."*

film with live sound, and I still cannot; this is because up until the last minute, and even while the scene is being filmed, I will intervene, give advice or orders, and throw life belts to the actors; and also because the cast often consists of two, three, maybe six different nationalities, speaking different languages and dialects. Another reason is that it is not true that actors always have the right voice, or that their voice fits their face: if I have already changed an actor, dressed and made him or her up differently, and altered his gestures and the way he smiles, why should his voice be sacrosanct, when a different voice could make the character more disturbing, surprising or profound? In *La dolce vita* and in *8½*, for instance, I was tempted to dub Marcello Mastroianni: I would have liked to give him a more hysterical, ambiguous voice, as his own seemed flat to me, lacking in resonance and depth, with no vibration, no falsetto.

By the time I begin the dubbing, the film editor's secretary has already taken a sort of copy from the soundtrack. I have to rewrite all the dialogues, adapting the actors' lines to the movement of their lips. In other films, these things are done by specialists, but in mine I have to do it myself. I sit down in front of it and write, and the dubbers stand there watching in alarm: in a serious film-making establishment I would be stopped, whereas in Cinecittà they accept it and put up with me. I select only a few actors as my dubbers, four or five of the very best, and always the same people, and I give them several parts each. The most impressive was Alighiero Noschese. He was phenomenal, an unparalleled example of the flair and the mediumistic gift of the actor, a prodigious mimic who could absorb like radar phonetic impressions of people. One evening, in a restaurant in Fregene, I saw myself on a television screen talking.

Deeply disconcerted by this, I looked myself in the eye: it was my eye, so it must be my idea that I was hearing. I had a shattering realization: Noschese could capture your soul as well as your voice – he was an empty space ready to adopt any shape or form. If he were still around, I would have had him dub my voice instead of dubbing it over my own, as for

example in *Intervista*: I felt ill at ease, whereas dubbing is a kind of yoga or Zen requiring a highly controlled spontaneity such as one should probably adopt in everyday life as well.

While the dubbing is being completed, the so-called effects track is made. This assembles all the noises needed in the film: wind, cars colliding, a volley of gunfire, tyres screeching round a bend. Specialist technicians arrive with their effects library, small cases containing pre-recorded tapes of every conceivable noise, a repertoire which often ends up not being used at all. Other specialists look after the domestic noises like doorbells and footsteps. My relationship with these specialists is often tricky, involving a mixture of respect and diffidence. Specialization generally strikes me as an attitude of mind in which the detail becomes as important as the whole. I am slightly irritated by this kind of restricted vision, which is sometimes a bit obtuse and presumes to be scientific. Detail invoked and justified simply in the cause of realism is of no use at all in my films; in fact, it often gets in the way.

*F*rom E la nave va. *Opposite: the scene in which the symbolic rhinoceros shut up in the hold of the ship is winched up onto the deck and washed with hoses. Right: a drawing by Fellini and (above) the lifeboat of refugees heading through a sea made of plastic, from which the head of special effects chief Adriano Pischiutta has just emerged. But the real sea played its part too, in trick-shots and montage sequences. "I filmed the sea at every moment of the day and night. I wanted a sea capable of expressing feelings, a threatening sea, one that brings news of fateful events; I wanted a sea in which the water is invisible, like a block of ice; or a somber, black sea that could even terrify a mysterious creature rising up from its depths. It is not easy to find a sea that is so expressive. We got through miles of film."*

The sound made by a pair of shoes, recorded and dubbed simply because on the screen you can see someone walking along, does not add anything. It spoils the aural dimension of the scene and nothing else, unless that treading sound has a particular meaning and becomes significant as a snatch of music or a line of dialogue can. I leave out a large number of sounds from the effects tracks of my films, and if this absence threatens to destabilize the sound of the voices, then ''Dr Fellini's airwaves'' take care of everything.

At this point the film is into its final stage. Relationships improve, there is a relaxed atmosphere, and things go smoothly. Then comes the most enjoyable job of all, overlaying the music. In the early days, with the composer Nino Rota, I used to look for particular pieces of music I am fond of and cheer me up, and which help to give the camera a dance rhythm. I found in Nino Rota a thoroughly likeable and congenial working partner: he wrote some of the most memorable and typical music for my films, and yet he never managed to see the films themselves first. Nino had always managed to remain in a world of perpetual childhood, treating everything with trust and awe, with the enchanted smile of a sensitive infant in a perpetual, gentle daydream; the dimming of the lights had the same effect on him that it has on newborn babies: he went straightaway into a deep, peaceful, undisturbed sleep. He would wake up when the lights were turned on again, and say: "Why have you turned the lights on?" "Because the film is over." "Already?" he would reply, "I haven't seen anything yet . . ." I did not mind. He was an angel, Nino Rota. His tendency to fall asleep was in no way a criticism, but rather the way a baby would. Even during lunch, just before the dessert, he would already have started to stare at his glass, and then, like a baby who is replete with milk, he would suddenly drop off. His creative time was at dusk. Then, as though he were in touch with another world – he had the fixed gaze of a medium – he only needed a few clues and could come up with the most extraordinary results: the entire score for $8\frac{1}{2}$ was written in three, possibly four days at the most. I would

*S*tills *from* Ginger e Fred (Ginger and Fred, *1985), a film which among other things expresses a mocking hostility to the culture of television and its rituals. The aging pair of dancing partners is reunited at the invitation of a television programme. In the photographs: Ginger and Fred dancing; the television dancers; applause for the hero and heroine (Giulietta Masina and Marcello Mastroianni).*

tell him what was happening in the film, explain what feeling I needed to arouse, and he, in the way he responded, seemed to draw out of me something which really existed already inside me. He gave you the impression that you had created the music yourself.

But apart from in my work, I prefer not to hear music: it affects me, disturbs me, I get taken over by it and so protect myself by rejecting it and running away like a thief from an open safe. I do not know, perhaps this is Catholic conditioning again: the fact is that music makes me feel melancholy, and I get overwhelmed with feelings of remorse; so, like remorse, it is of no use to me – it sounds a warning, which destroys you because it fills you with yearning and regret for a world of harmony, peace and courtesy from which you have been excluded, even banished.

Of opera I know little. For me, opera is something deeply and mysteriously Italian; I have no wish to become involved with this obscure force, which has the power to devour and dumbfound you. Clearly, there is in me a resistance to being swept up by such a whirlwind or to exposing myself to the great tidal wave of operatic emotion. I have often been asked to produce opera, but I have always said no; I do not see what more a film director could give to a piece of theater which is already complete in itself. The disordered element opera has, making it uncertain, temporary and chaotic, the kind of happening which is created by an orchestra, conductor, singers and audience coming together, seems complete to me. I also think that the mistakes, dissonances and flat notes are an integral part of this creation. This too is part of opera's charm. The presence of a producer is completely superfluous. It would be like getting someone to direct the *bersaglieri*, running full tilt with a fanfare and plumes fluttering in the wind, or a Catholic procession. For me, however, discovering those great cathedrals of music erected by the genius of Verdi was an extraordinary experience.

In *E la nave va*, I unashamedly made use of, and even went so far as to manipulate, some arias by Verdi which I had listened to in the past without paying much attention. I first came across them as a child, when the woman who came

*P*hotographs of the filming of Intervista. *Above: Fellini in front of the set built for the screen tests of a film within a film, based on Kafka's novel* America. *Right: Fellini with the dancers in an advertisement, majorettes escorting a golden cannon which fires lipstick at the poster of a woman's* mouth. *Several members of Fellini's regular cast took part in the film, playing themselves: they included director of photography Tonino Delli Colli, executive producer Piero Notarianni, and Fellini's secretary Fiammetta Profili.*

Marcello Mastroianni: pictures from La dolce vita, *the first of Fellini's films he appeared in, and the first time he took on in the cinema the identity or at least the appearance of his director. Twenty-six years later, the character returns to double for Fellini again. Fellini appears in* Intervista *as himself. Mastroianni plays him too. But the actor is also seen in the film as Mandrake, the thirties cartoon wizard created by Lee Falk and the artist Phil Davis. But magic here has become pragmatic: Mandrake/Mastroianni is working on a soap powder commercial.*

to do the washing sang *La Traviata* and the electrician who mended our front door bell intoned, *"Di quella pira l'orrendo fôco,"* and then the mattress-maker would sigh, *"Di quell'amor, di quell'amor che è palpito . . ."* Opera has always seemed to me like a fundamental part of Italian life. It is like the sound of church bells ringing for Mass on Sundays, or the sitting rooms of middle-class houses; it is part of the very fabric of our society, and we have grown up and been educated with it to the point where we feel the same about opera as we do about proverbs: we have heard them so many times that they have lost their power and their symbolic meaning. We do not actually hear them anymore.

While the music for the film is being taped, all the magnetic and sound tapes arrive in the editing suite. The noise tracks alone can add up to twenty, and there might be sixty tracks in all. Each in its own channel, they are all condensed in the mix, and a single track is produced from them. I take part in this task of constant selection and condensing until it is complete. This is the jumbo jet taking off, the final stage.

Then the laboratory prints copies of the film. I go with the projectionist to check the first print. Invariably I hear the same complaints, every time without fail: "Colder, hotter, there's too much magenta, what the hell have you done with this blue? Is that face supposed to have measles? Too much red!" I then listen to the excuses, which are also always exactly the same: "So many planes flying overhead, the vibrations . . . Yes, but last night we were down to ten below zero, I knew it would end up like that, I told you so . . ."

I ask two or three friends of mine to the first screening. They are always the same ones, people I can trust; I know that they will tell me they like it, no matter what. Having turned off the light and adjusted the sound, I usually go and have a look round the projection room, chat with the operators there, every now and again taking a look through the little window and catching sight, as though by chance,

of my film down there, a long way away, on the screen, as it begins to work its seduction. Or I go out, while the screening goes on. I sit on the steps leading up to the projection room, and my presence is detected at a distance by the dogs who at night become the masters of Cinecittà.

A shot from 8½.

HISTORY
by Mario Lombardo

29 January 1936

Building work on Cinecittà began at nine o'clock in the morning. The foundation stone was laid by Benito Mussolini. This center for the Italian film industry was erected on a site between the seven- and nine-kilometer markers on the Via Tuscolana, on the Roman plain. The site (144 acres) was obtained from a limited company selling building land. It was never ascertained if it had belonged to Prince Torlonia or to the Vatican.

28 April 1937

At five o'clock in the afternoon, Mussolini performed the opening ceremony of Cinecittà. It had been built in 475 days by Carlo Roncoroni to a design by the architect Gino Peressutti. The Duce was present as shooting began on the films *Elevazione*, for which Vittorio Mussolini had written the script, *Il feroce Saladino*, starring Angelo Musco, *I misantropi*, and *Aviazione*, which was under the overall direction of Vittorio Mussolini. The Duce also watched the synchronization of *Scipione l'Africano*, directed by the distinguished Italian composer Ildebrando Pizzetti.

1938

The Fascist government ordered that the importing of films from abroad be brought under the control of a state monopoly. The major American film companies withdrew from the Italian market in protest. With Metro-Goldwyn-Mayer, Twentieth Century Fox, Paramount and Warner Brothers out of the way, Italian cinema increased its own productivity, even recouping the eighty per cent which had been the American companies' share.

1943

After the collapse of the Fascist regime (25 July) and the arrest of Mussolini, Cinecittà's days seemed numbered, and its 1,200 employees were sacked and paid off, interrupting work on the films in the process of being made at that time: *La freccia nel fianco* directed by A. Lattuada; *Che distinta famiglia* by G. Bonnard; and M. Soldati's *Daniele Cortis*. Between April 1937 and July 1943, 279 films had been made at Cinecittà: of these, 120 were comedies, 17 war or propaganda films; and 142 in other categories (opera, historical films, thrillers etc.).

1944

During January there were heavy Allied bombardments. Part of Cinecittà was damaged, and it was also occupied by German troops, who vacated it (on 4 June 1944) when the Allied Forces entered Rome. The Allied Control Commission and the International Refugee Organization took over the disused film center and turned it into a refugee camp. In November, Lattuada completed his film *La freccia nel fianco* at Palazzo Lazzaroni in Rome. It was the first Italian film to be completed after the armistice, having been started at Cinecittà.

1947

The Italian film industry was brought under the responsibility of Giulio Andreotti, then undersecretary to the President of the Council. His first official act was to freeze a percentage of the income of foreign film companies earned in Italy (the so-called "frozen assets"). American film companies were thus forced to produce their films in Italy, particularly so as to be able to recoup these assets they could not take out of the country.

1950

Mervyn LeRoy began filming *Quo vadis ?*, paving the way for the first American film era in Italy. Foreign film stars came to Rome, and the myth of Via Veneto quickly grew. Between 1950 and 1965, 27 films were made at Cinecittà, epic not only in content but also in the size of their budgets.

1958

Cinecittà was no longer owned by the state and came under the administration of the Ministry of State Economic Participation as a self-governing film corporation. In addition, a government body (Italnoleggio) was created to manage film distribution.

1967

The start of the second American film era in Italy. This time, it arose because of the crisis in the cinema in the United States itself and the closure of many of the studios in Hollywood. It also marked the period when a lot of Italian "B" pictures were made, in particular spaghetti westerns. This second American era was to last until about 1971.

1976

Opening of the new developing and printing laboratory at Cinecittà. The center had, however, reached a crisis: it had thirteen film studios, and little more than 300 employees. The producers involved were the state film distribution company Italnoleggio on the one hand, and Radiodiffusione italiana (RAI, the state television company) on the other.

Surrounded by a thick, high wall, its rectangular buildings set well apart from each other among pines, flower beds and tree-lined paths, a quiet place where you can hear only the muffled roar of the traffic in the distance and bird song overhead, at first sight Cinecittà could conceivably appear to be a hospital or a rather grand nursing home.

To begin with, it is the setting which creates this image, but once you have passed through the gates and entered the compound, closer inspection makes the whole idea even more feasible. Some of its buildings are low and glass-fronted: they have been built using man-made materials, plastic, ABS, anodized aluminium, in rather gentle pastel shades of china blue and sea green. They are elongated edifices, rather like out-patients' departments or research laboratories; and from them, appropriately enough, emerge distinguished-looking men in white coats and half-moon spectacles, white-haired, their faces pink and reassuring, or thin and reflective, with a measured, relaxed bearing and a confident gait, talking to each other in muted voices as befits the quiet around them. Often they will walk about in pairs along the tree-lined avenues, with their immaculate white coats billowing out behind them, acknowledging in a dignified way the greetings of others, responding to some with light-hearted gestures of solidarity, but always composed and self-possessed. The building they are leaving is the developing and printing department (directly to the left as you enter the enclosed area of Cinecittà) beneath the shade of age-old pine trees, together with lush oleander and pittosporum bushes; and the gentlemen in the white coats you have caught sight of could be Giacomo Volpi and Renato Serafini, colour technicians known to everyone and courted by everyone because it is on their skill that the success of the print depends, its brightness, and its fidelity to the colour tones of the film which has just been shot.

But there are also other technicians here who wear a white coat, those who look after exposures or baths or the cutting of the negative, the washes and the screenings; and in this "uniform" they derive a certain prominence by belonging to a section of the staff which, though not actually connected with health and hygiene, looks that way to the unsuspecting visitor who still thinks he sees doctors, nurses and ambulance men there.

For the women it is different, because their long coats are pink, with a small white collar, sometimes worn unbuttoned at the top for added flair. They go past in a hurry, often wearing Scandinavian-style clogs, or, like Signora Maria, they go about their business gliding elegantly up and down the moving walkways of the section. They look less like nurses than luxury attendants, there not for the care of patients but more broadly for the smooth running of the whole operation: making up rooms, tidying, changing linen, replenishing all the accessories, equipment and essentials. I picture them alongside gigantic trolleys (which they often actually are) piled high with table linen, sheets and cleaning agents.

When they stroll along the avenues, with their coats casually thrown over their shoulders, the image is complete: where else could they be going except from one part of a well-organized hospital to another?

The deception of these coats does not stop there. Other technicians (those who do make-up for example) have blue coats, like radiologists. Signor Penza, who is responsible for titles, and has styled his hair like a round, flat loaf on top of his head, really does look like a radiologist. Possibly sensing this resemblance which brings him distinction, he never takes his coat off for a moment; it would not be surprising if he wore it over his overcoat. Signor Penza has the bearing of a chief physician because, being the head of his section, he is never alone: the other two technicians, also in blue coats, follow close behind him, with a genuine air of respect, smiling quietly at him to show they have understood the incomprehensible aphorisms which he will occasionally utter. One of the assistants is from Urbino and in all probability is still there in spirit, under those transcendental medieval towers, so far is he removed from his work, from the room he occupies, and even from Rome where he has lived for at least thirty years.

When the radiologists meet up with the doctors, there are gentle signs of lethargic recognition; or, if they get together at the door to the restaurant, there is a polite exchange of courtesies, "after you, no after you," which is never overdone, and has no a hint of obsequiousness.

The modern prefabricated department of developing and printing is so peaceful, quiet and unobtrusive, (there is nobody on the door, no noise, no groups chatting or standing around), that once past the first courtyard of the penitentiary, the Cinefonico building promises some fun and a bit of a hullabaloo. There is always an air of cheerfulness, there, for no particular reason, a light-headed feeling of lizards basking in the sun.

The old Cinefonico building is one of those little wards where you are comfortable, the food is good and there are only a few patients. So there is also less discipline, nobody wears a long coat, and good-natured rogues will willingly linger on the stairs to indulge in a bit of idle back-biting. It is difficult to walk past the front of the Cinefonico and not find someone on duty there outside the door at the top of the steps. If the sun is shining, there will be somebody sitting on the steps or half stretched out on the travertine slabs to either side. The atmosphere in this section is exactly what you find in those buildings in a hospital which were put up before the others: no matter how many restorations and new coats of paint, you can never relate them to the most recent extensions. That is how the people who work there treat the place; they too have the air of old soldiers recruited at the first draft, and occupy the rooms in the same way that one would wear an old pair of slippers.

It is good to walk past the Cinefonico in the certain knowledge of being greeted by the nurse on duty. There is also a small parking place facing the door, and some people leave their cars there, no matter which part of Cinecittà

they then have to get to; clearly, they realize that when both coming and going they will have a chance to have a chat there, and learn something useful.

If the weather is fine, then the huddle of people is sure to be there, moving mysteriously to and fro, indoors and out; they all go in, and they all come out again, always together, and always with that air of gratuitous cheerfulness, a bit of a spring in the step and a swaying of the body. At the center of the huddle you can often see the Senior Nurse in his turtle-neck pullover, his light blue eyes wide open as though the world is a never-ending wonder and he an aging schoolboy. The ward is his and you can see why: he has more say than any doctor or chief physician answerable to the management. Everyone calls him, and everyone looks for him; it is obvious that without him you will not get a decent bed, nor a good meal, to say nothing of other extras. He has that aura about him of organized anarchy, which is such a common feature of the public services in Italy, where a coffee at the bar with the right person carries more weight than an application in writing. But having said that, everything runs very smoothly, and even with a certain display of efficiency: the member of staff who stays in the office looks just like a reception clerk, with his register and even a computer screen. He is a kindly, sober individual whose eyes smile at you from behind gold-rimmed glasses; he is sympathetic and accommodating, almost afraid to contradict, like someone used to handling patients with special needs – they may be disturbed, they may even be insane. And so this aspect of a psychiatric clinic begins to peep through, promising some truly mad scenarios.

The Cinefonico is right next to the bar, or the store as it is called in barracks and prisons. Here the peaceful nursing home suddenly comes to life; it would be closer to the truth to say it fills with people, because a quick glance discovers no real sign of actual liveliness or dynamism, but rather a lingering about, the way fish do in a fountain, a gentle floating around and opening of mouths with no other aim in mind.

It is especially when the bar is closed and so no longer looks like a bar at all, that the disorientated wandering, the casual formation of groups that follows no known logic, brings very much to mind the scene in the garden of a convalescent home. There is a seemingly endless amount of time to be filled, and nothing to fill it with but meals, very infrequent medical inspections, and protracted therapy sessions, a difficult stretch of time you can do nothing to help pass except by taking it steady, like treading with slow and thoughtful steps along the seabed. The overall effect of this group of individuals in pyjamas – or so they appear if you continue to regard them in this particular light – or in dressing gowns with their shoes and socks on, has something aquatic about it. The same effect occurs when the groups break up, much as fish do, only to regroup almost unchanged a bit nearer or farther away, according to the currents perhaps, or the insects on the surface which they can only reach by darting up as quick as a flash.

The greatest pleasure for these patients in their dressing gowns is to stand in the middle of the tree-lined avenues right in the path of the few vehicles that pass forcing them to adjust their pace accordingly to the slow movements of the pedestrians; a gap opens, but barely wide enough to let the vehicles through, and is then closed up again at once with an air of irritated indifference.

Here the impression of lunacy becomes more tangible because if the imagination pictures individuals in pyjamas, the reality goes way beyond that. The groups along these avenues, some standing still, others moving, are likely to be wearing fantastic costumes which give a more detailed indication of the type of mental disturbance involved: you can see Admiral Lord Nelson, one of Savonarola's monks, the scruffy soldier at the head of an invincible army carrying a wooden sword like children do, a seventeenth-century prostitute, and a female rock singer in tights, often mingling with ordinary patients dressed in chequered shirts and fustian breeches. It is not uncommon to see in the midst of this motley bunch the doctors in their white coats and the radiologists in their blue. Then the party livens up, someone gesticulates; somebody else gets a slap, and they all burst out laughing. And on days when the hot wet sirocco is blowing, and the air among the pine trees is humid and incandescent, charged with electricity, small fights can break out just like that, with build-ups of raucous yelling. In these situations the inmates resemble animals in a herd in which incomprehensible aggression might be unleashed like a bolt of lightning, to the accompaniment of enraged or pitiful cries. But this comparison with animals and the zoo is another view of Cinecittà, and we will come back to that.

Outside the bar, then, there is only a disconsolate loitering, a waiting for something, a summons, a chance, a pretext for everyone to move to somewhere else. Outside there are no benches, and as the place does not have fixed opening hours, the patients will often sit on the bar steps to kill time, clearing the odd patch of mud, pine needles, cigarette ends and pine cones left there by the wind or by mistake, and starting up card games with the usual crowd standing round to watch. Someone lights a cigarette, someone else leafs through a newspaper until he gets to the sports page; then the looks become more intense as the soccer match, the results, the goals or the tactics entice them out of the stupor of their catatonic state. They are all talking at once and the more excited they become, the louder their voices grow, with doctors and nurses being called upon to take sides, which they only too readily do, glad to be involved in these therapeutic exploits.

Meanwhile the hospital as a whole carries on its normal, mysterious life as before. Other coats are seen strolling along the avenues, or suddenly appearing round the corner of a large building, shouting something. Sometimes, because the site is so large, people use bicycles, tricycles or wheelbarrows to get about. Recently they have also introduced fork lift trucks, those small mechanical tractors which are used to lift weights and clear obstacles. Of the objects they carry best it is better to say nothing: it would appear that the disturbed inmates here devote all their energies to building the most crazy toys, particularly when it comes to judging proportions. There are skittles as high as three-storey apartment blocks, castles with spires on top, oases with palm trees, entire Parthenons, the Nike of Samothrace, the treasure chest of Drake the Pirate, a galleon flying the skull and crossbones, and even a pig's trotter as high and as large as Rome's main railway station.

The staff in white coats have the task of transporting these cumbersome playthings from one place to another; and when they are no longer any use to anybody, they are dumped on the edge of the enclosed area in a field, usually near the large open-air swimming pool which looks like a dry dock or launching bay that has been practically forgotten by everyone.

The staff who are responsible for the inmates' creativity therapy can be distinguished from the others by the colour of their coats, which are either grey or brown, depending on whether the activity is with iron or wood.

The carpenters wear brown coats, the machine shop staff grey ones. Manual work is strongly encouraged at all levels; this can be seen from the large quantity of timber, frames and softwood joists which are continually being loaded and unloaded. It is not a heavy task, because the process is carried out at a very easy-going pace, so that nobody gets out of breath or anxious and is kept almost happy, often whistling or singing, in fact, with the serene inspiration of artists. The materials are never particularly valuable – clearly, these people are only playing at what they are doing – but the results are often stunning. This is one of the reasons why, as the therapy is so obviously beneficial, but without over-indulging the patients' egos too much, two words have been put up in elegant, fairly large lettering on a pair of machine shops, set back a bit and less conspicuous than the other buildings: MODELLING and SCULPTURE.

On the strength of this message, whoever is shut in there to work feels reassured by the nobility of the category of their efforts, and can comfortably leave the present famous landmarks in order to explore in art: the Greece of Phidias and Praxiteles, the Florence of the Medici.

Outside the workshops, in fact, you can find a bit of everything, especially statues which are invariably very large but some also life-size, standing up, stretched out, on their backs in the field, and heaped one on top of the other. And inside the workshops, which derive their light from the skylights in the roof, the work is clearly fast and furious, using stucco and plaster of Paris, but also plastic casts, moulds and mock-ups.

When demand is heavy, that is to say, when there are a very large number of patients wanting to work, then some are assigned to projects which involve building entire villages, one or other of the hills to either end of the grounds being chosen as the site.

To look at the results, you would think they were genuine works of architecture, complete with roads, colonnades, shops, house fronts, dry-stone walls, belvederes, piazzas, fountains and bell towers. Whole teams are employed on these building programmes and each individual has his job to do: painting, stucco-work, decorating and repairing. There are glaziers, road men, masons, electricians, fresco artists and carpenters. Working alongside each other, they build real, brilliant monuments that are admired by everyone, as illusory and as impassioned as the ghosts which created them.

The realizing of these fantasies seems to have an extremely good effect, giving substance to concepts, dimensions to the imagination. Perhaps, too, these creations reveal in forms which are recognizable and no longer threatening, the deviations of a mind oppressed by a surfeit of ravings.

At meal-times everyone goes to the restaurant. Outside the low glass-fronted building you will often find a cheerful and impatient queue; the aroma of the food wafts out and envelops everyone. There is a slight thrill of anticipation. Luckily the queue moves forward quickly, thanks to three servers who are always happy and smiling and know how to treat the patients. One of the three is a plump and full-bodied woman, vaguely resembling a customs officer. Quick and generous, she holds out ladlefuls of pasta and soup like someone who believes fully and absolutely in the food and its goodness, and also in quantity and the benefit to be had from a good meal. She holds out the steaming plateful, sprinkled with cheese, and moves on to gratify the next person in the queue. The other servers do likewise – they are less plump but no less warm and motherly, with the second courses, the meat, the vegetables, the cheese board, encouraging, attentive, never in a hurry, never ill-mannered. They call almost everyone by their first name, they never force you to choose something, they recommend the dishes that have come out best, and they use sign language. If there is a surprise, a new dish, something original and out of the ordinary, they offer it promptly but without salesmanship. And a tray is soon filled up, ready to be carried to one of the white, spotless tables, but not forgetting the water, the wine or the beer or almost any other drink being discreetly offered by a Neapolitan server with a true Neapolitan nature, melancholy but cheerful and philosophical. This touch of pre-prandial Neapolitan culture is like the final ingredient towards a good meal – this representative of the intestine of Italy (Naples, geographically speaking, can be found about that far down) seems to preside like a tutelary deity over the patient's digestion, favouring a happy outcome for his mastication and the processing of his nourishment. Every diner is despatched, tray in hand, with a holy sign, blessing and exorcizing them. It is bestowed with a benign smile, and a knowledge which you cannot define but which nevertheless belongs to a very specific and identifiable wisdom.

Patients, doctors, and rogues alike, go to their places happy and serene, ready to pay tribute to the food which has the incomparably beneficial power to unite the individual with the primary concern of life.

After the restaurant, a visit to the bar. This has been refurbished and with its black rubber floor, it instantly seems to blend in with the overall hospital image of the place. The barmen, Walter and Franco (frank in name and in nature), are to all intents and purposes nurses, transferred purely for servicing reasons to this paramedical responsibility of serving at the bar counter. They sell drinks and coffee to a clientele of connoisseurs, an unchanging group of customers who take coffee in an obsessive daily ritual. The universe which is created here is also vaguely segregated, prison-like, modelled round movements and actions which are always the same and can thus be seen as maniacally defensive distinguishing features. Here at the bar people are called by their name in time-honoured tradition, and there is much hanging about in huddles, gangs and small groups; it is a kind of free territory, a stretch of border country where a degree of exchange is conducted and allowed with the outside world in the form of visitors, suppliers and occasional observers. As a result the bar is packed, taken literally by storm every time it opens, and every time it closes, when the patrons have to dolefully tear themselves away. The bar represents the harbour, the crossroads, the gateway to the Orient, a meeting point and a point of diaspora, a place for hiring people, a rendezvous, a sounding board for information of every sort, a labyrinthine bazaar trading in people, objects and services. At the bar is where the telephones are and where money flows, and in fact it is the only place anywhere in the establishment where it is possible to spend and purchase, where money circulates as it does in the outside world, where contact with that world becomes real, concrete, and less illusory and clouded than in any other corner of the enclosure.

Of the two bar-tending nurses, Walter, the older one, is always smiling, accommodating, diplomatic; he lavishes coffee on you as if it were the elixir of life, with the most extravagant of negotiations which far from tiring him reinforce the measure of his priestly largesse. His clear, innocent eyes shine with a smile which is totally spiritual and conciliatory, a smile expecting warmth in return, at every request: coffee in a glass, in a cup, with extra hot water, short and strong, hot, boiling, ready to drink, with a splash of milk, with froth on top, with liqueur added, a double, a triple, in a large cup, with sugar, without, in a thermos, in a small bottle, in plastic cups . . .

The same applies to a *cappuccino*, Campari, freshly squeezed orange or grapefruit juice, Babycham, brandy, Amaroaverna and Sambuca. The orders arrive in a deafening hubbub, delivered out in a bold voice, shouted, whispered, signalled, pointed to, with a catch-phrase, by name, by metaphor, in an arrogant or moderate, respectful or high-handed way; and all these orders find their way to Walter's ear, his immediately receptive glance and his infallible but not ingratiating memory where he remembers what everyone has, how everyone likes it and what everyone's poison is.

Walter is an old nurse who knows a thing or two about his patients; so does Franco, though he is younger, not so good-natured, not so involved. Franco evaluates them: he administers smiles, allocates them in accordance with a private assessment of his own based on selection, on what they're worth, how important they are and how likeable. Franco has not gone grey yet, and perhaps he never will.

At the cash desk sits Nadia, silent, unalterable in her rhythms and moods, to witness the exuberant routine that whirls about her from opening to closing time, day in and day out.

At the bar too there is an internee, possibly a former patient who, as happens in isolation establishments, has not managed to get away from the protective enclosure, get beyond the door, pass through the gates and fling himself into the outside world. So he is allowed within the walls, and inevitably into the bar, that stretch of border country, on an

incredible commercial pretext: he sells books. Every day he sets up a small stand on one of the formica-topped tables, or on a couple of chairs, a crate, or an empty packing case, wherever a flat surface offers him a place to display his goods; and there he will wait patiently for the customers who never come.

The bookseller is called Polverini and he has the face of a freed man who has no more baths to run nor gourmandizers' feasts to prepare; his eyelids lowered over reddish eyes, a general downward movement that is echoed in all his facial muscles. With his tall stature, curvature of the spine, scarf, worn-out loden overcoat, the battered boots on his large feet — when you see him in the morning from behind, hurrying to his imaginary place of work in the bar and carrying the blue plastic carrier bag with his lunch, he reminds you of Jacques Tati, the genius Tati who died in poverty, and equally of all the clowns who can no longer make anyone laugh. You would want to buy all his books from him, in one go, in a faint-hearted act which would, however, leave him without "work" and the patients without his company, such a useful presence and one so integrally part of an incurable condition. And the books? What kind of books are they? They are unsold stock, improbable titles, remainders of series which did badly, publications which went to the wall, anthologies for children who never came to buy them and are only interested in watching cartoons on television.

However, they are books, merchandise, and they are evidence of a hidden, parallel activity, conducted in the shadow of the wards and the casemates and the overbearing warehouses – the black market.

At Cinecittà, they sell everything, even specializing in certain lines. There are those who sell casual clothes, like Vinicio, and other boutique fashions; leatherware is a separate activity, with belts and bags; and then there are perfumes of any brand or provenance; for designer articles, you only have to ask. You know who to go to for wrist watches and bracelets, who handles gold and precious stones; there is a choice of smokers' accessories; if it isn't in stock, they can order it for you. A radio? A portable television? How much do you want to spend, when do you want it for?

This sort of trading is not even worth mentioning, since it can be found in any enclosed institution, like some down-market complement to the consumerism in the outside world, a picturesque and also slightly wretched re-offering of the styles and status symbols which are given recognition in that society beyond the walls. What you would not be expecting, on the other hand, is another kind of produce on offer, so unlikely, in fact, that it gives the enclosed world of Cinecittà a fable-like quality. There is a hole in the wall of the enclosure, near the swimming pool; through this narrow opening, if you call him, a certain Nello will appear, a country bumpkin, ugly as a face on a tarot card, carrying little baskets of eggs which are still warm and pigeons, guinea-fowl, spring chickens, ducks and turkeys which have all been well fed. When he is not free, Vitaliana or Martina (his daughters, or maybe his mistresses) appear instead and take all the orders for eggs and poultry that come from the other side of the wall.

It seems almost idyllic, an acre of Arcadia evoking the spirit of Virgil's nature poetry which is by no means alien to the district. The large number of meadows, fields and green spaces foster the bucolic spirit and are conducive to contact with rural life. Nature here is spontaneously generous, as you can discover just by looking down on the ground, and if you know how to recognize tasty rocket salad in the field or plain wild chicory, you can gather whole bundles of them here. Some of the sound technicians are particularly keen on this relaxing hobby, while others concentrate instead on mushrooms, pine seeds and poplar saplings, picking and collecting in abundance. Some pick up pine cones and pine seeds by the sackful; others go looking for snails when the flower beds are sodden after heavy showers of warm rain. And there are others for whom nature's spontaneity is still not enough; so they get what they want by creating little gardens, or, even more imag-

inatively, cultivating fruit trees. Where, though? Anywhere, of course: this kind of manual work and the contact with the earth, fruits and seeds symbolize in themselves the acquiring of health, equilibrium, and a road to salvation. A man who comes from the land knows by instinct where to find the very stuff of the universe, and when he is troubled, he goes back to the bosom of the earth, to its refuge and slow heartbeat.

In the administration of this country hospital, one cannot overlook those who are employed in management and support services. There are quite a few of them here. They are in no way out of place and are very much part of the whole exercise. They go to make up important infrastructures. Cinecittà, believe it or not, even has its own vehicle repair workshop. It is there to keep the directors' cars (in the plural, you notice) in good running order, and there is a mechanic whose sole job it is to do just that. There is also a co-op, not in the sense of a workers' association, but a grocery store where you can stock up at favourable prices on a range of goods such as could be found in any supermarket. Most of those who shop here use it for pasta, sugar, detergent and pre-packed food; and at Christmas and Easter, they buy their traditional *torrone* (nougat), *panettone* (fruit-bread) and *colomba* (dove-shaped Easter cake) here.

The secretaries and other female members of staff in the administration see this co-op as an obligatory port of call and a legitimate pretext for a stroll and a chat. They go to shop there in groups of three or four walking side by side so that they spread right across the avenue. They make a show of it, like models parading on a catwalk, or a Sunday promenade down the main street of their village, so as to be seen and receive compliments, veiled suggestions and invitations from the male employees on their way back from the bar who eye them up while lighting their break-time cigarettes. During these chance encounters, there is an exchange of furtive glances and knowing smiles; they will make a tacit rendez-vous in the archives, that out of the way corridor, or in the room of a colleague off sick, away from prying eyes. But, as in village life, there are no possibilities for privacy or secrecy. Everyone knows everything about everyone else, there is a mounting buzz of confidences, a tireless, excited murmuring like the sound of the cicadas on summer nights in the great pine trees. Then there is the woman who is considered to be more beautiful than the others and who becomes a source of interest to all the men; and so you see her changing, day after day, in response to the particular desire she has aroused: her hair is shinier, and is worn down to her shoulders; ever tighter leather skirts accentuate the movement of her backside as she walks; and there is, overall, a sense of haughtiness about her body language, breasts proud and challenging, face held high and almost impassive, the slight arch of the eyebrow aquiver with promises which are immediately disavowed, and the reluctant, rather tense smile conceded with sovereign disdain. A most noble and notable attitude which often proves absolutely inappropriate to the person concerned, who passes unnoticed in a different, less coercive world.

Sometimes these strolls, the exodus from the offices, lead to the tennis courts, which are real and not part of any film set, complete with showers and changing rooms. The players who make their appearance here are, on occasion, pallid-looking individuals, a bit green about the gills, short of breath, on the fat side because their work is mainly sedentary, their eyes blinking at the sudden brightness of the daylight. These are the film editors, the movieola assistants, who have escaped from the captivity of a job which keeps them cooped up in rooms without windows. They move about as though drunk with this excess of glare, unable to get used to it, visibly ill at ease; and as soon as they are able to go inside again, or the break for fresh air is over, they are quite willing to let themselves be sucked back into their shadowy dens, into a few cubic meters of cigarette smoke, body odour and the acidic smell of film.

If, particularly in the summer, you go past the building where the movieolas are, you may suddenly hear piercing screams and yells shattering the quiet. You can never be sure if it is the film editors doing the screaming or their editing equipment, on which they wind and unwind out miles and miles of story, sometimes beautiful stories, imprisoned by magic in a transparent roll and a magnetic tape. The film editors see themselves as their custodians, all are dreamily touched by their tragedy; almost all of these editors bear a grievous wound, their faces set in pained sympathy with destinies to whose secrets they alone hold the key.

It is the kind of work pathologists and surgeons do, this cutting-up, which perhaps allows no room for merriment or chaos, and which, it seems, the hospital here cannot do without.

Closeted in their cubbyholes with capricious, tyrannical directors, whose flights of fancy they are obliged to stitch together endlessly, the editors experience fascination and outrage while avoiding any personal judgement, suspending their own critical faculty altogether.

One of these film editors is nicknamed "roly-poly" because he has a natural tendency to podginess; some time ago, with a resigned though also gratified expression on his face, he showed off to his colleagues the love bites which a woman producer had given him in the privacy of the editing suite.

This mixed bag of behavioural traits, bordering on the pathological, the apparent orderliness and tranquillity of the surroundings, resembling in this respect too a real nursing-home, makes it justifiable and legitimate to have guards on site, security men vigilantly ready to intervene.

These are well-built young vigilantes dressed American-style in black trousers, black leather jackets with conspicuous metal plates on them, mirror sunglasses and large, clearly visible pistols in holsters hanging from their waists.

When you first see them at the entrance, they seem like warders at an Oklahoma state penitentiary, even though the guardroom they are watching you from (until recently, anyway; now the "image" is a little more up to date) looks like the usual cross between an interview room at a police station and the waiting room at a railway station. Nevertheless, they are pistol-carrying lads – a bit overweight, a bit pasta-bellied, and a bit too good-natured. A new generation of security man is coming in now, more neurotic, thinner, with shining eyes, chewing gum. They are playing a role they have learned by heart, under the influence of too many television films; their presence makes the point unequivocally that their "patch" here is privileged and protected territory, an enclosed area one may not enter without authorization, a permit or a pass. A Black Maria would look very much in place at the entrance gates; but then so would an ambulance with its sirens blaring.

Nor would it be against the grain to come across the Mercedes of one of the chief physicians there, a comfortable, well-sprung limousine with smoked-glass windows and inside, just barely visible, a face to be guessed at and gazed upon fondly, the woman who at long last seems to look like what you have always suspected a real woman should look like, right there and yet at the same time inaccessible, closed up in her beauty but also exposed, exhibited, inviting, capable of casting secret spells under the influence of which even a common mortal, even a security man, maybe at one time or another, given the opportunity, fate, good fortune, a moment of caprice, sensuality or bewilderment, a little self-assurance just at the right moment . . .

The big lads with their black leather jackets and pistols stuck in their belts, withdraw deferentially, step back attentively, even giving a sign of salute, a half bow, as the Mercedes purrs quietly through, reflecting streaks of sky, trees and foolish smiles in the broad sweep of its windows. Behaviour is very different, however, to the point of arrogance, when their waiting room contains young girls looking for walk-on parts in a film. Then our boys become gun-toting

angels, guarding the gates of paradise. They make a show of knowing everyone, greeting those passing through with exaggerated familiarity, as though they were comrades in arms with them. The young girls, sheathed in jeans which they can hardly move in, swaying along on very high heels, unaware of the fact that they are not actually Giorgio Armani models who weigh under ninety pounds and are six feet tall, overwhelmed by the dark intoxication of being allowed into the barracks, succumb to the fascination of the uniform, and see the young man on guard duty as a more than useful ally for their purposes, an accomplice, the ferryman to get them across. So they turn on languid, promising, suggestive, brazen, cunning smiles; and the guardroom, for some inexplicable reason, immediately takes on a shady appearance, like a brothel.

The other day three or four of these big security lads were in Adriana's room. One was sitting down, pale faced, while Adriana was trying to stick a plaster over his eyebrow (Adriana can always supply a plaster, a cup of coffee, a good word, especially for the male species who she secretly regards as marvellous, incapable creatures in need of care like helpless children, amusing and, above all, a species to be protected). The others were standing round, watching this first-aid treatment, getting in the way and unable to help:
"You should have got him in the eye!"
"Should have smashed his face in, more like!"
"But what did he do?"
"He didn't get into a punch-up with a drunkard, did he?"
"You should have just fired at him!"

Heroically, the man with the plastered eyebrow was calming his nerves, making light of the incident and covering over his traces like a true policeman:
"I just banged into a door, it's nothing . . ."
"Didn't you say it was a pine tree?" asked Adriana, beaming.
"Door, pine tree, who cares?"

A drunk had been pestering somebody in the bar. Nadia at the cash desk telephoned through to security. The big lads arrived, and the moment he caught sight of them, the drunk seemed to calm down, let himself be escorted from the bar, but once outside protested at being physically restrained, wriggled free looking grim-faced and irritated, and threw a punch at the nearest of the guards, a blind swipe in the air which caught the young security man full on the eye. Luckily, the lad reacted sensibly: he slumped to the ground but did not start to get angry, let alone go berserk or even give a thought to the pistol in his holster. The drunk blathered on, and the other guards bent over their colleague and got him back on his feet. The incident was closed. At Cinecittà everyone knows everyone else: wasn't he one of the Boss's extras, this drunk? In the morning, or that very night, the matter would be left in his hands.

The drunk, gesticulating, staggering about, stopping to get his balance and then lurching off again, has reached the gates of the enclosure unescorted. He already knew that, because of what he did, this is the last time he would ever darken the door of Cinecittà. He would be crossed off, banished, banned. The security guards forgive but the Boss never forgives.

At one time the security men used to be called patrolmen and they did their rounds on bicycles. They were ex-police officers or ex-military police, extremely trustworthy, always on hand, and never showy or exhibitionistic. They used to wear shapeless leather coats almost to their knees, in which they were protected against everything; draughts, wind, snow, fog and rain, their faces furrowed by very deep lines, weatherbeaten like the bark of trees; their strong, gnarled hands gripping their handlebars, purple in winter from the cold, and inevitably unsuited to precision jobs requiring manual dexterity. They had generous-looking, clear, trustworthy eyes like large dogs have. And indeed the dogs at Cinecittà, who had found a safe haven and resided here, used to follow this patrol on its leisurely circuits like a pack of hounds behind their leader, obediently but also protectively. This pack took their pace from the unhurried pedalling motion of the patrol, and went wagging their tails, with no discipline in the ranks, along the tree-lined avenues, circling the studios, sniffing the air, barking if some danger signal took them by surprise in their daily routine of surveillance. And when the patrolman got off his bicycle to go into the long corridors of the store houses, poorly lit by the glimmer of the duty light, the dogs went in with him, nosed around the padded doors, stretched their necks up the stairwell leading to the upper floor, and carefully checked out trails which had been left by somebody at some time but which were no longer of any interest.

These days the security men are trained on rifle ranges, to be ready for anything. They tour the avenues of Cinecittà on high-powered Hondas, communicate via walkie-talkie sets, get quickly out of their small Renault 4s that are covered in white and blue stickers, patrol the site with fraught efficiency, men of few words, their minds on something else, indifferent to the big dogs trying with little success to keep up with them.

And then, as it used to be, the dogs follow at the heels of some old caretaker, who has no Honda, no Renault 4 or leather jacket with badges on it, but rides an old bicycle, doing the rounds at a leisurely pace, checking out the studios, the departments, the stores, pedalling as far as the farthest store houses, the open spaces where sets are built, and to the swimming pool. The dogs maneuver in a group, sometimes leading the bicycle, sometimes alongside it, and every now and then falling behind perhaps for the simple, tempting reason that they could then suddenly overtake in one exhilarating run, barking into the air. They know that in a short while they will be the only ones left inside Cinecittà, lords of all they behold, meadows, trees, office blocks, entrusted, just like that, with the huge responsibility of guarding the entire establishment. Once the last visitor has gone, as have the last of the workmen and the projectionists, these docile, affectionate, mild creatures, as playful as ragamuffin clowns, are transformed, so the guards say, into the fiercest of beasts, ready to pounce on anyone, constantly on the alert, never sleeping, always suspicious. Even a bitch who has had endless litters and drags her sagging teats along the ground, and heavy and jostled by her pups, will, when dusk falls, once again become an intrepid and vigilant guard dog through the night.

The wind blows along the avenues at Cinecittà. It is the Roman sirocco, a humid, odorous wind. It has reached this far after crossing the center of Rome, sweeping through houses and courtyards, swirling among the granite ruins, piazzas, obelisks and arches, billowing into vast cathedrals fragrant with incense, ruffling the tops of trees and houses, spreading through the dormitory towns in the suburbs, and so into the countryside beyond, past sheep cotes and the crumbling remains of tombs, aqueducts, mausoleums, towers, finally colliding with the barrier of hills and entwining itself round its own currents inside the walls of this strange sleeping prison. Here it plunders the avenues in a rush of air, and the litter and drink cans and pine needles are picked up by the wind, the pine cones are sent rolling, the bushes bending from the force of it, the high branches of the pines and the dark shoulders of the cypresses leaning sideways, as it whistles through the porches and moans along the long studio corridors, tearing material from scaffolding in fierce gusts which set black plastic sacks flapping noisily. And the dogs, with their noses in the air, smell everything that the wind brings with it, stretching their necks to its scents, blinking their eyes and twitching their nostrils all the time. Who knows what they are picking up on the breeze.

This is the time for ghosts. They say there *are* some at Cinecittà, that they can be heard in the administration block, on the other side of the vast meadow facing the entrance, the sort of building which looks as though it has been assembled from a child's construction kit, box-houses in coloured wood put together in a rather uninspired way, with building-block simplicity. And yet the ghosts like this building, for it is there that they hold their get-togethers, amusing themselves through pastimes, evidence of which reaches those on duty in the guard-room nearby in the form of unexplained shivers. They are noises of a night life which ought not to be there: clear footsteps, rustles, squeaks, the strange sounds of doors, cupboards and drawers shutting, and ringing voices. Presences. They get talked about during the day as calmly as befits a harmless phenomenon which is also common knowledge; by its very nature, the place will always have something of the suspense of a magic enclosure where ghosts are somehow at home. The alchemy of images carried out here daily, the power of suggestion (like hallucinations, visions and hypnotic projections) unleashing psychotic materializations, nightmares, double takes and mirages, provides the basis for believing in a parallel world which lives and breathes, as Jung said, behind a sheet of carbon paper and which every now and again, simply through a shift in dimension, envelops us, mesmerizing us momentarily. Phantoms. The place allows them in, and welcomes them. And why should they not be there?

Nadia talks about these things. She is a gentle-mannered little lady, all dressed in white, from her coat, which has a vaguely military look to it, to her light wool dress with the little round collar and dropped waist, her fishnet stockings also white, and cream-coloured shoes of soft leather. To look at her, it is hard to judge her age, with make-up on her porcelain-like face, and her hair, which is thirties-style, in blond ringlets as perfect and neat as a doll's wig.

She was running some old Italian newsreels through the movieola when, there on the faded screen she saw, with the aid of a powerful lamp, more ghosts appear: these were real specters, images of the dead, famous women film stars, distinguished actors, politicians of the Fascist regime, producers, set designers, scene painters, who were no longer living. A long strip of film was actually entitled "The Ghosts of Cinecittà" and, using an ingenious dissolving technique in which figures emerge from paintings or walk through walls and doors, it told the comic story of two ghosts who happen to find themselves included quite by chance in the production of a film.

Ghosts lead to more ghosts; magical, arcane presences which our senses perceive as mingling together without definition. What is this sudden evidence of a transparent world, this airy vapour from the Underworld which envelops us so unthreateningly, invites us to linger a while, stay with it, perhaps even pass through the white mist of the screen? And why exactly is Nadia, a graceful, innocent ghost herself, the sentinel of this crossroads, and guardian of these shadows?

It is here, Fellini tells us, in this department that Cinecittà keeps a sense of its own past, the memories of itself; and are not the Muses or art itself daughters of Mnemosyne and Jupiter?

So, when the dogs are once again curled up of an evening in the warm meadows swept by the sirocco, their paws curled up under them, and they stretch their necks, their sensitive nostrils aware of something out there in the darkness which we would not have noticed, you ask yourself: who knows what they are picking up on the breeze?

And then you realize that maybe you already have an inkling.

FILMOGRAPHY

1937
DOTTOR ANTONIO (Il), Guazzoni
DUE MISANTROPI (I), Palermi
ERAVAMO SETTE SORELLE, Mattoli
FELICITÀ COLOMBO, Mattoli
FEROCE SALADINO (Il), Bonnard
LASCIATE OGNI SPERANZA, Righelli
LUCIANO SERRA PILOTA, Alessandrini
MAZURKA DI PAPÀ (La), Biancoli
NAPOLI D'ALTRI TEMPI, Palermi
PIETRO MICCA, Vergano
PRINCIPESSA TARAKANOVA (La), Ozep-Soldati
STASERA ALLE II, Biancoli
ULTIMI GIORNI DI POMPEO (Gli), Mattoli
VOGLIO VIVERE CON LETIZIA, Mastrocinque

1938
BATTICUORE, Camerini
CASA DEL PECCATO (La), Neufeld
CASTELLI IN ARIA, Genina
CAVALIERE DI SAN MARCO (Il), Righelli
DUE MADRI (Le), Palermi
EQUATORE, Palermi
FUOCHI D'ARTIFICIO, Righelli
GIUSEPPE VERDI, Gallone
HANNO RAPITO UN UOMO, Righelli
LOTTE NELL'OMBRA, Gambino
MA L'AMOR MIO NON MUORE, Amato
MARCHESE DI RUVOLITO (Il), Matarazzo
MARIONETTE, Gallone
NAPOLI CHE NON MUORE, Palermi
OROLOGIO A CUCÙ (L'), Mastrocinque
PARTIRE, Palermi
PER UOMINI SOLI, Brignone
RICCHEZZA SENZA DOMANI, Poggioli
STELLA DEL MARE, D'Errico
TERRA DI FUOCO, L'Herbier-Ferroni
TERRA DI NESSUNO, Baffico
ULTIMO SCUGNIZZO (L'), Righelli
VOCE SENZA VOLTO (La), Righelli

1939
ALBUNA MESSIAS, Alessandrini
ARDITI CIVILI, Gambino
ASSEDIO DELL'ALCAZAR (L'), Genina
ASSENZA INGIUSTIFICATA, Neufeld
AVVENTURA DI SALVATOR ROSA (Un'), Blasetti
BIONDA SOTTOCHIAVE, Mastrocinque
CARMEN TRA I ROSSI, Neville
CARNEVALE DI VENEZIA (Il), Adami-Gentilomo
CONQUISTA DELL'ARIA (La), Marcellini
DOCUMENTO (Il), Camerini
DORA NELSON, Soldati
EDUCANDE DI SAINT-CYR (Le), Righelli
ERAVAMO SETTE VEDOVE, Mattoli
FORNARETTO DI VENEZIA (Il), Bard
GRANDI MAGAZZINI, Camerini
IMPUTATO, ALZATEVI!, Mattoli
LAMPADA ALLA FINESTRA (Una), Talamo
LO VEDI COME SEI?, Mattoli
MANON LESCAUT, Gallone
MILLE CHILOMETRI AL MINUTO, Gallone
MONTEVERGINE, Campogalliani
NOTTE DELLE BEFFE (La), Campogalliani
PICCOLO HOTEL, Ballerini
PICCOLO RE, Romagnoli
RETROSCENA, Blasetti
SOGNO DI BUTTERFLY (Il), Gallone
TRAVERSATA NERA, Gambino
UOMO DELLA LEGIONE (L'), Marcellini
VALIDITÀ GIORNI DIECI, Mastrocinque

1940
ABBANDONO, Mattoli
ADDIO, GIOVINEZZA!, Poggioli

ALLEGRO FANTASMA (L'), Palermi
AMAMI, ALFREDO!, Gallone
ANTONIO MEUCCI, Guazzoni
CAPITAN FRACASSA, Coletti
CORONA DI FERRO (La), Blasetti
DON PASQUALE, Mastrocinque
ELISIR D'AMORE (L'), Palermi
FORZA BRUTA (La), Bragaglia
GERLA DI PAPÀ MARTIN (La), Bonnard
ISPETTORE VARGAS (L'), Franciolini
MANOVRE D'AMORE, Righelli
MARCO VISCONTI, Bonnard
MELODIE ETERNE, Gallone
NASCITA DI SALOMÉ (La), Choux
OLTRE L'AMORE, Gallone
ORIZZONTE DIPINTO, Salvini
PECCATRICE (La), Palermi
PICCOLO ALPINO, Biancoli
PIRATI DEL GOLFO (I), Marcellini
POZZO DEI MIRACOLI (Il), Righelli
ROMANTICA AVVENTURA (Una), Camerini
ROSE SCARLATTE, De Sica-Amato
SAN GIOVANNI DECOLLATO, Palermi
SENZA CIELO, Guarini
SOGNO DI TUTTI (Il), Biancoli-Kish
TUTTO PER LA DONNA, Soldati
UOMO DEL ROMANZO (L'), Bonnard

1941
ANIME IN TUMULTO, Del Torre
BEATRICE CENCI, Brignone
BENGASI, Genina
BOCCA SULLA STRADA (La), Roberti
CATENE INVISIBILI, Mattoli
CENA DELLE BEFFE (La), Blasetti
COMPAGNIA DEI MATTI (La), Pratelli
DUE TIGRI (Le), Simonelli
FRA DIAVOLO, Zampa
MARITI (I), Mastrocinque
MERCANTE DI SCHIAVE (Il), Coletti
ORE 9 LEZIONE DI CHIMICA, Mattoli [9 O'CLOCK
    CHEMISTRY LESSON]
ORO NERO, Guazzoni
PIA DE' TOLOMEI, Pratelli
PILOTA RITORNA (Un), Rossellini
PIRATI DELLA MALESIA (I), Guazzoni
PROMESSI SPOSI (I), Camerini
REGINA DI NAVARRA (La), Gallone
SANCTA MARIA, Neville-Faraldo
SE IO FOSSI ONESTO, Bragaglia
SE NON SON MATTI NON LI VOGLIAMO, Pratelli
SISSIGNORA, Poggioli
TERESA VENERDÌ, De Sica
TRE RAGAZZE VIENNESI, Marischka-Fatigati
TURBAMENTO, Brignone
ULTIMO BALLO (L'), Mastrocinque
USURAIO (L'), Hasso

1942
ADDIO AMORE, Franciolini
AMICO DELLE DONNE (L'), Poggioli
AVANTI C'È POSTO, Bonnard
BELLA ADDORMENTATA (La), Chiarini
BISBETICA DOMATA (La), Poggioli
CANAL GRANDE, Robilant
CONTESSA CASTIGLIONE (La), Calzavara
DUE CUORI TRA LE BELVE, Simonelli
DUE ORFANELLE (Le), Gallone
FORNARINA (La), Guazzoni
FEDORA, Mastrocinque
FUGA A DUE VOCI, Bragaglia
GENTE DELL'ARIA, Pratelli
HARLEM, Gallone
INFERNO GIALLO (L'), Radwany
LUISA SANFELICE, Menardi

MAESTRINA (La), Bianchi
MALOMBRA, Soldati
MARIA MALIBRAN, Brignone
MASCHERA E IL VOLTO (La), Mastrocinque
MATER DOLOROSA, Gentilomo
MORTE CIVILE (La), Poggioli
NON TI PAGO, Bragaglia
NOSTRI SOGNI (I), Cottafavi
ODESSA IN FIAMME, Gallone
QUATTRO PASSI TRA LE NUVOLE, Blasetti [FOUR
   STEPS IN THE CLOUDS]
QUELLI DELLA MONTAGNA, Vergano
SENZA UNA DONNA, Guarini
SORELLE MATERASSI (Le), Poggioli
STORIA D'AMORE (Una), Camerini
UOMO DALLA CROCE (L'), Rossellini
VIE DEL CUORE (Le), Mastrocinque
ZAZÀ, Castellani

1943
APPARIZIONE, De Limur
CAPPELLO DA PRETE (Il), Poggioli
DONNA DELLA MONTAGNA (La), Castellani
ENRICO IV, Pastina
FIORE SOTTO GLI OCCHI (Il), Brignone
FRECCIA NEL FIANCO (La), Lattuada
LOCANDIERA (La), Chiarini
MONTE MIRACOLO, Trenker
NON SONO SUPERSTIZIOSO, MA!, Bragaglia
T'AMERÒ SEMPRE, Camerini
TI CONOSCO MASCHERINA, De Filippo
TRISTI AMORI, Gallone
VIAGGIO DEL SIGNOR PERRICHON (Il), Moffa

1947–1948
CUORE, Coletti [HEART AND SOUL]
FABIOLA, Blasetti
PRINCE OF FOXES (The), Henry King
SEPOLTA VIVA (La), Brignone
ULTIMI GIORNI DI POMPEI (Gli), L'Herbier [THE
   LAST DAYS OF POMPEI]

1949
AMORI E VELENI, Simonelli
BACIO DELLA MORTA (Il), Brignone
BEAUTÉ DU DIABLE (La), Clair
CIELO SULLA PALUDE (Il), Genina [HEAVEN OVER
   THE MARSHES]
DONNE SENZA NOME, Radvany [UNWANTED
   WOMAN]
SANTO DISONORE, Brignone
YVONNE LA NUIT, Amato

1950
PORTEUSE DU PAIN (La), Cloche
QUO VADIS?, Le Roy [QUO VADIS]

1951
ABRACADABRA, Neufeld
ALTRI TEMPI, Blasetti [INFIDELITY/IN OLDEN DAYS]
BELLISSIMA, Visconti
BUON VIAGGIO POVER'UOMO, Pastina
CITTÀ SI DIFENDE (La), Germi [PASSPORT TO HELL]
DON CAMILLO, Duvivier [THE LITTLE WORLD OF
   DON CAMILLO]
LIGHT TOUCH (The), Brooks
MESSALINA, Gallone [THE AFFAIRS OF MESSALINA]
OLIVA, INCANTESIMO TRAGICO, Sequi
UMBERTO D, De Sica
VENDETTA DEL CORSARO (La), Zeglio [DUAL
   BEFORE THE MAST]

1952
AIDA, Fracassi
AMORE ROSSO, Vergano
CAMICIE ROSSE, Alessandrini
CANZONI DI MEZZO SECOLO, Paolella

CARROZZA D'ORO (La), Renoir [THE GOLDEN
   COACH]
CIECA DI SORRENTO (La), Bomba
CROSSED SWORDS, Krims
DONNA CHE INVENTÒ L'AMORE (La), Cerio
FANCIULLE DI LUSSO, Vorhaus
FIAMMATA (La), Blasetti [PRIDE LOVE AND
   SUSPICION]
GIOVINEZZA, Pastina
HO SCELTO L'AMORE, Zampi
MONDO LE CONDANNA (Il), Franciolini [THE
   WORLD CONDEMNS THEM]
PRESIDENTESSA (La), Germi [THE LADY
   PRESIDENT]
PROCESSO ALLA CITTÀ, Zampa [A CITY ON TRIAL]
RITORNO DI DON CAMILLO (Il), Duvivier [THE
   RETURN OF DON CAMILLO]
ROMAN HOLIDAY, Wyler
STAZIONE TERMINI, De Sica
   [INDISCRETION/INDISCRETIONS OF AN
   AMERICAN WIFE]
SUL PONTE DEI SOSPIRI, Leonviola
UOMINI SENZA PACE, De Heredia
VIALE DELLA SPERANZA (Il), Risi
VIVA IL CINEMA, Trapani

1953
AMORI DI MEZZO SECOLO, Germi-Franciolini-
   Paolella-Chiari
CANZONI, CANZONI, CANZONI, Paolella
CAROSELLO NAPOLETANO, Giannini [NEAPOLITAN
   FANTASY]
CAPITAN FANTASMA (Il), Zeglio
CENTO ANNI D'AMORE, De Felice
CINEMA D'ALTRI TEMPI, Steno
COSE DA PAZZI, Pabst
DONNE PROIBITE, Amato [ANGELS OF DARKNESS]
GRAN VARIETÀ, Paolella
MATRIMONIO (Il), Petrucci
MIZAR, De Robertis [FROGMAN SPY]
NOI CANNIBALI, Leonviola
PAESE DEI CAMPANELLI (Il), Boyer
PRIMA DI SERA, Tellini
SCAMPOLO, Bianchi
TEMPI NOSTRI, Blasetti [A SLICE OF LIFE/ANATOMY
   OF LOVE]
UOMINI CHE MASCALZONI (Gli), Pellegrini
VESTIRE GLI IGNUDI, Pagliero
VIOLENZA SUL LAGO, Cortese
VITELLONI (I), Fellini [SPIVS/THE LOAFERS/THE
   YOUNG AND THE PASSIONATE]

1954
APPASSIONATAMENTE, Gentilomo
ARTE DI ARRANGIARSI (L'), Zampa
BAREFOOT CONTESSA (The), Mankiewicz
CAMILLA, Emmer
CASA RICORDI, Gallone
CASTA DIVA, Gallone
CHERI-BIBI, Pagliero
DIVISIONE FOLGORE, Coletti
DUE ORFANELLE (Le), Gentilomo
FORTUNE CARRÉE, Borderie
HELEN OF TROY, Wise
MADAMA BUTTERFLY, Gallone
PECCATO CHE SIA UNA CANAGLIA, Blasetti [TOO
   BAD SHE'S BAD]
SEDUTTORE (Il), Rossi
SINFONIA D'AMORE, Pellegrini
UOMINI OMBRA, De Robertis

1955
ADRIANA LECOUVREUR, Salvini
AMICHE (Le), Antonioni [THE GIRL FRIENDS]
AMICI PER LA PELLE, Rossi [FRIENDS FOR LIFE]

FORTUNA DI ESSERE DONNA (La), Blasetti [LUCKY
   TO BE A WOMAN]
ONOREVOLE PEPPONE (L'), Gallone [DON
   CAMILLO'S LAST ROUND]
PADRONE SONO ME (Il), Brusati
PO' DI CIELO (Un), Moser
PREZZO DELLA GLORIA (Il), Musu
SCAPOLO (Lo), Pietrangeli
TESORO DI ROMMEL (Il), Marcellini [ROMMEL'S
   TREASURE]
WAR AND PEACE, Vidor/Soldati

1956
BEATRICE CENCI, Freda
BOY ON A DOLPHIN (The), Negulesco
CITTÀ DI NOTTE, Trieste
FINESTRA SUL LUNA PARK (La), Comencini
LITTLE HUT (The), Robson
SCHIAVE DI CARTAGINE (Le), Brignone
SOGNI NEL CASSETTO (I), Castellani
SOUVENIR D'ITALIE, Pietrangeli [IT HAPPENED IN
   ROME]
SULLE STRADE DI NOTTE, Vasile
SUOR MARIA, Camerini
TEN THOUSAND BEDROOMS, Thorpe

1957
ANGELO PASO POR BROOKLYN (Un), Vajda [THE
   MAN WHO WAGGED HIS TAIL]
ANNA DI BROOKLYN, Denham-Lastricati [FAST
   AND SEXY]
BEN-HUR, Wyler
DIGA SUL PACIFICO (La), Clément [THE SEA
   WALL/THIS ANGRY AGE]
FAREWELL TO ARMS (A), Vidor
GIOVANI MARITI, Bolognini [YOUNG HUSBANDS]
ISLANDER (The), Wilson
LEGEND OF THE LOST TIMBUCTU, Hathaway
LOI EST LA LOI (La), Cristian-Jaque
MISTERI DI PARIGI (I), Cerchio
NOTTI BIANCHE (Le), Visconti [WHITE NIGHTS]
QUIET AMERICAN (The), Mankiewicz
VACANZE A ISCHIA, Camerini [ONE WEEK WITH
   LOVE]
VENERE DI CHERONEA, Tourjansky [APHRODITE,
   GODDESS OF LOVE]

1958
ERODE IL GRANDE, Tourjansky [HEROD THE
   GREAT]
GIUDITTA E OLOFERNE, Cerchio [HEAD OF A
   TYRANT]
MORTE VIENE DALLO SPAZIO (La), Heusch-Bava
   [DEATH COMES FROM OUTER SPACE]
NUN'S STORY (The), Zinnemann
PIA DE' TOLOMEI, Grieco
SOLITI IGNOTI (I), Monicelli [PERSONS
   UNKNOWN/BIG DEAL ON MADONNA STREET]

1959
ARCHIMEDE, Francisci
BACCANALI DI TIBERIO (I), Simonelli
CARTAGINE IN FIAMME, Gallone [CARTHAGE IN
   FLAMES]
CONTESSA AZZURRA (La), Gora
COSACCHI (I), Tourjansky [THE COSSACKS]
DOLCE VITA (La), Fellini [THE SWEET LIFE]
ET MOURIR DE PLAISIR, Vadim [BLOOD AND
   ROSES]
GENERALE DELLA ROVERE (Il), Rossellini
IT STARTED IN NAPLES, Shavelson
LEGIONI DI CLEOPATRA (Le), Cottafavi [LEGIONS
   OF THE NILE]
MESSALINA, Cottafavi
NOTTI DI RASPUTIN (Le), Chenal [NIGHTS OF
   RASPUTIN]
ROSSETTO (Il), Damiani [RED LIPS]

STRADA DEI GIGANTI (La), Malatesta
VENTO DEL SUD, Provenzale

1960
AMORI DI ERCOLE (Gli), Bragaglia
ARGONAUTI (Gli), Freda
BACCANTI (Le), Ferroni
BRIGANTE (Il), Castellani
CHE GIOIA VIVERE, Clément [WHAT JOY OF LIFE]
COME SEPTEMBER, Mulligan
DONNA DEI FARAONI (La), Tourjansky [THE PHAROAH'S WOMAN]
ERA NOTTE A ROMA, Rossellini
FRANCESCO OF ASSISI, Curtiz [FRANCIS OF ASSISI]
MULINO DELLE DONNE DI PIETRA (Il), Ferroni
REGINA DELLE AMAZZONI (La), Sala
RELITTO (Il), Cacoyannis [THE WASTREL]
REVAK THE REBEL, Maté
ROMANOFF AND JULIET, Ustinov
SAFFO, VENERE DI LESBO, Francisci [THE WARRIOR EMPRESS]
SICARIO (Il), Damiani
ULTIMO DEI VICHINGHI (L'), Gentilomo [THE LAST OF THE VIKINGS]
VIVA L'ITALIA, Rossellini

1961
ASSEDIO DI CORINTO (L'), Costa
CLEOPATRA, Mankiewicz
DAMON ET PYTHIAS, Bernhardt
DON CAMILLO MONSIGNORE, Gallone
ERCOLE AL CENTRO DELLA TERRA, Bava [HERCULES IN THE CENTRE OF THE EARTH]
ERCOLE ALLA CONQUISTA DELL'ATLANTIDE, Cottafavi [HERCULES CONQUERS ATLANTIS]
GOLIATH CONTRO I GIGANTI, Malatesta [GOLIATH AGAINST THE GIANTS]
JESSICA, Negulesco [JESSICA]
LYCANTHROPUS, Benson [I MARRIED A WEREWOLF]
MACISTE, L'UOMO PIÙ FORTE DEL MONDO, Leonviola [THE STRONGEST MAN IN THE WORLD]
ORAZI E CURIAZI, Young [DUEL OF CHAMPIONS]
PONZIO PILATO, Rapper
SOGNI MUOIONO ALL'ALBA (I), Montanelli-Craveri-Gras
VANINA VANINI, Rossellini [THE BETRAYER]

1962
ATTICO (L'), Puccini
CARMEN DI TRASTEVERE, Gallone
FLIGHT FROM ASHYA, Anderson
IO, SEMIRAMIDE, Zeglio
MARE MATTO, Castellani
MONACA DI MONZA (La), Gallone
PATRIARCHI DELLA BIBBIA (I), Baldi
PERSEO L'INVINCIBILE, De Martino [PERSEUS AGAINST THE MONSTERS]
PINK PANTHER (The), Edwards
ROGOPAG, Rossellini-Gregoretti-Pasolini-Godard
VENERE IMPERIALE, Delannoy

1963
CARDINAL (The), Preminger
CORRUZIONE (La), Bolognini
FALL OF THE ROMAN EMPIRE (The), Mann
LIOLÀ, Blasetti
LONG SHIPS (The), Cardiff
MACISTE ALLA CORTE DELLO ZAR, Anton [GIANT OF THE LOST TOMB]
PREDONI DELLA STEPPA (I), Anton [THE MIGHTY KHAN]
QUESTO MONDO PROIBITO, Gabella
VENDETTA DELLA SIGNORA (La), Wicki
VISITA (La), Pietrangeli

1964
AGONY AND THE ECSTASY (The), Reed

ANGELIQUE ET LE ROI, Borderie
ANGELIQUE, MARQUISE DES ANGES, Borderie [ANGELIQUE]
BELLE FAMIGLIE (Le), Gregoretti
CASANOVA 70, Monicelli
CENTO CAVALIERI (I), Cottafavi [THE HUNDRED HORSEMEN]
DOMINATORE DEL DESERTO (Il), Anton
EL GRECO, Salce
ERIK IL VICHINGO, Caiano [VENGEANCE OF THE VIKINGS]
GIULIETTA DEGLI SPIRITI, Fellini [JULIET OF THE SPIRITS]
LUNGHI CAPELLI DELLA MORTE (I), Margheriti [THE LONG HAIR OF DEATH]
QUESTA VOLTA PARLIAMO DI UOMINI, Wertmüller
RIVINCITA DI IVANHOE (La), Anton
SAUL E DAVID, Baldi
SFINGE SORRIDE PRIMA DI MORIRE (La), Tessari
VON RYAN'S EXPRESS, Robson

1965
AGENTE 077 DALL'ORIENTE CON FURORE, Grieco [FROM THE ORIENT WITH FURY]
AGENTE 077 MISSIONE BLOODY MARY, Grieco [MISSION BLOODY MARY]
AGENTE X-1-7 OPERAZIONE OCEANO, Anton
CACCIA ALLA VOLPE, De Sica [AFTER THE FOX]
CAST A GIANT SHADOW, Shavelson
DUE MARINS E UN GENERALE, Scattini [WAR ITALIAN STYLE]
FANGO SULLA METROPOLI, Wilson
JUDITH, Mann
NEW YORK CHIAMA SUPERDRAGO, Paget [NEW YORK CALLED SUPER DRAGON]
PER QUALCHE DOLLARO IN PIÙ, Leone [FOR A FEW DOLLARS MORE]
QUESTIONE D'ONORE (Una), Zampa [A QUESTION OF HONOUR]
TERRORE DALLO SPAZIO, Bava [PLANET OF THE VAMPIRES]
THREE COINS IN THE FOUNTAIN, Negulesco
TRENTA WINCHESTER PER EL DIABLO, Baldanello
UOMO CHE RIDE (L'), Corbucci [THE MAN WITH THE GOLDEN MASK]
UOMO DI TOLEDO (L'), Martin [CAPTAIN FROM TOLEDO]

1966
ANNA MOFFO SHOW, Lanfranchi
BIGGEST BUNDLE OF THEM ALL (The), Annakin
BOBO (The), Parrish
COME RUBARE UN QUINTALE DI DIAMANTI IN RUSSIA, Reed
DUE FIGLI DI RINGO, Simonelli
DUE MAFIOSI DELL'F.B.I. (I), Bava
DUE SANCULOTTI (I), Simonelli
FISCHIO AL NASO (Il), Tognazzi
HAREM (L'), Ferreri
JOHNNY YUMA, Guerrieri
OPERAZIONE SAN GENNARO, Risi [THE TREASURE OF SAN GENNARO]
RESA DEI CONTI (La), Sollima [THE BIG GUNDOWN]
SETTE CINESI D'ORO, Cashino
SETTE MONACI D'ORO, Girolami
SPARA FORTE, PIÙ FORTE . . . NON CAPISCO, De Filippo
TEXAS, ADDIO, Baldi [THE AVENGER]
THREE BITES OF THE APPLE, Ganzer
WANTED, Ferroni

1967
ANGELIQUE ET LE SULTAN, Borderie
ARRIVA DORELLIK, Steno
AVVENTURIERO (L'), Young [THE ROVER/THE ADVENTURER]
BUONA SERA, MRS. CAMPELL, Frank

CJAMANGO, Mulargia
FERMATE IL MONDO, VOGLIO SCENDERE, Cobelli [STOP THE WORLD, I WANT TO GET OFF]
GIORNI DELL'IRA (I), Valerii [DAYS OF ANGER]
HOUSE OF CARDS, Guillermin
INDIFFERENTE (L'), Lizzani [INDIFFERENCE. Episode from LOVE AND ANGER]
INDOMPTABLE ANGELIQUE (L'), Borderie
MARITO È MIO E L'AMMAZZO QUANDO MI PARE (Il), Festa Campanile
NON SCOMMETTERE LA TESTA COL DIAVOLO, Fellini [TOBY DAMMIT. Episode from TALES OF MYSTERY]
OCCHIO SELVAGGIO (L'), Cavara
OPERAZIONE SAN PIETRO, Fulci
QUESTI FANTASMI, Castellani [GHOSTS ITALIAN STYLE]
ROMEO E GIULIETTA, Zeffirelli [ROMEO AND JULIET]
TENDERLY, Brusati [THE GIRL WHO COULDN'T SAY KNOW]
TRENO PER DURANGO (Un), Caiano
UOMO, L'ORGOGLIO, LA VENDETTA (L'), Bazzoni

1968
ADVENTURERS (The), Gilbert
ADVENTURES OF GERARD, Skolimowski
BASTARDI (I), Tessari [SONS OF SATAN]
BATTAGLIA DI EL ALAMEIN (La), Ferroni
CADUTA DEGLI DEI (La), Visconti [THE DAMNED]
CATHERINE, IL SUFFIT D'UN AMOUR, Borderie
C'ERA UNA VOLTA IL WEST, Leone [ONCE UPON A TIME IN THE WEST]
CHIEDI PERDONO A DIO NON A ME, Davis
LADY HAMILTON-ZWISCHEN SCHMACH UND LIEBE, Christian-Jacque [EMMA HAMILTON]
MATRIARCA (La), Festa Campanile [THE LIBERTINE]
SCUSI, FACCIAMO L'AMORE?, Caprioli
SECRET OF SANTA VITTORIA (The), Kramer
SHOES OF THE FISHERMAN (The), Anderson
STORY OF A WOMAN, Bercovici
STRAZIAMI MA DI BACI SAZIAMI, Risi
TEPEPA, Petroni

1969
ALTRE (Le), Falley
BATTAGLIA D'INGHILTERRA (La), Castellari [BATTLE SQUADRON]
CERTO, CERTISSIMO, ANZI PROBABILE, Fondato
COLPO ROVENTE, Zuffi
CON QUALE AMORE, CON QUANTO AMORE, Festa Campanile
CONTESTAZIONE GENERALE, Zampa
DOUBLE FACE, Freda
INAFFERRABILE INVINCIBILE MR. INVISIBILE (L'), Margheriti [MR SUPERINVISIBLE]
INFANZIA, VOCAZIONE E PRIME ESPERIENZE DI GIACOMO CASANOVA, VENEZIANO, Comencini
INVASIONE (L'), Allegret
MEDEA, Pasolini
PISTOLERO DELL'AVE MARIA (Il), Baldi
PUSSYCAT PUSSYCAT I LOVE YOU, Amateau
RANGERS (I), Montero
SASSO IN BOCCA (Il), Ferrara
SATYRICON, Fellini [FELLINI-SATYRICON]
STATO D'ASSEDIO (Lo), Scavolini
TULIPANI DI HARLEM (I), Brusati
VIVI O PREFERIBILMENTE MORTI, Tessari

1970
ARCIERE DI FUOCO (L'), Ferroni
CITTÀ VIOLENTA (La), Sollima [VIOLENT CITY]
CLOWNS (I), Fellini [THE CLOWNS]
COSE DI COSA NOSTRA, Steno
DEBITO CONIUGALE (Il), Prosperi

GATTO A NOVE CODE (Il), Argento [THE CAT O'NINE TAILS]
LAST REBEL (The), McCoy
LEONARDO DA VINCI, Castellani
MADDALENA, Kawalerowicz
MORTE A VENEZIA, Visconti [DEATH IN VENICE]
NINÍ TIRABUSCIÒ, Fondato
PIANETA VENERE, Tattoli
SACCO E VANZETTI, Montaldo [SACCO AND VANZETTI]
SCIPIONE DETTO ANCHE L'AFRICANO, Magni
SPLENDORI E MISERIE DI MADAME ROYALE, Caprioli
STAGIONE ALL' INFERNO (Una), Risi
STATUE (The), Amateau

1971
AVVENTURE DI PINOCCHIO (Le), Comencini
BELVE (Le), Grimaldi
CLASSE OPERAIA VA IN PARADISO (La), Petri [THE WORKING CLASS GOES TO HEAVEN]
DIARIO DI UN ITALIANO, Capogna
LOVE STRESS, Lenzi
MORTADELLA (La), Monicelli [LADY LIBERTY]
ORLANDO FURIOSO, Ronconi
QUANDO LE DONNE PERSERO LA CODA, Festa Campanile
ROMA, Fellini [FELLINI'S ROMA]
SALOMÈ, Bene

1972
AMARCORD, Fellini
COLONNA INFAME (La), Risi
DELITTO MATTEOTTI (Il), Vancini
. . . E DI SHAUL E DEI SICARI SULLA VIA DA DAMASCO, Toti [OF SAUL AND THE ASSASSINS ON THE ROAD FROM DAMASCUS]
LUDWIG, Visconti
POPPEA, UNA PROSTITUTA AL SERVIZIO DELL'IMPERO, Brescia
RAGAZZA DALLA PELLE DI LUNA (La), Scattini [SEX OF THEIR BODIES]
SETTE SCIALLI DI SETA GIALLA, Pastore [LITTLE CRIMES OF THE BLACK CAT]
TOSCA (La), Magni
VILLEGGIATURA (La), Leto [BLACK HOLIDAY]
VITA A VOLTE È DURA, VERO PROVVIDENZA? (La), Petroni
VOGLIAMO I COLONNELLI, Monicelli
WHAT?, Polanski

1973
ALLONSANFAN, P. and V. Taviani
AMORE E GINNASTICA, D'Amico
INVENZIONE DI MOREL (L'), Greco
LIBERA AMORE MIO, Bolognini
MOSÈ, De Bosio [MOSES]
MUSSOLINI ULTIMO ATTO, Lizzani [THE LAST FOUR DAYS]
POLVERE DI STELLE, Sordi
PORTIERE DI NOTTE (Il), Cavani [THE NIGHT PORTER]
SISTEMO L'AMERICA E TORNO, Loy [I FIX AMERICA AND RETURN]
SOSPETTO (Il), Maselli
TEMPO DELL'INIZIO (Il), Di Gianni
ZANNA BIANCA, Fulci [WHITE FANG]

1974
ANNO UNO, Rossellini [ITALY YEAR ONE]
CASO RAOUL (Il), Ponzi
CORRUZIONE A PALAZZO DI GIUSTIZIA, Aliprandi
COUNT OF MONTE CRISTO (The), Greene
ETÀ DELLA PACE (L'), Carpi
FRATELLO (Il), Mida
IRENE IRENE, Del Monte
NON SI SCRIVE SUI MURI A MILANO, Maiello

NOVECENTO, Bertolucci [NINETEEN HUNDRED]
QUATTRO DELL'APOCALISSE (I), Fulci
RITORNO DI ZANNA BIANCA (Il), Fulci
SALVO D'ACQUISTO, Guerrieri
TERMINAL, Breccia

1975
ALTRO DIO (L'), Bartolini
CADAVERI ECCELLENTI, Rosi [ILLUSTRIOUS CORPSES]
CASANOVA, Fellini [FELLINI'S CASANOVA]
CASSANDRA CROSSING (The), Pan Cosmatos
CUORE DI CANE, Lattuada
DON MILANI, Angeli
GAROFANO ROSSO (Il), Faccini
LINEA DEL FIUME (La), Scavarda
QUANTO È BELLO LU MURIRE ACCISO, Lorenzini
SALÒ, Pasolini [120 DAYS OF SODOM]
SIGNORE E SIGNORI BUONANOTTE, Comencini-Loy-Magni-Monicelli-Moser-Scola
TODO MODO, Petri

1976
AL DI LÀ DEL BENE E DEL MALE, Cavani [BEYOND EVIL]
ALTRA METÀ DEL CIELO (L'), Rossi
ANTONIO GRAMSCI, Del Frà
CUORE SEMPLICE (Un), Ferrara
DESERTO DEI TARTARI (Il), Zurlini [THE DESERT OF THE TARTARS]
DOVE VOLANO I CORVI D'ARGENTO, Livi
GENIO (Il), Pinoteau
GIORNO DELL'ASSUNTA (Il), Russo
LUNGA STRADA SENZA POLVERE (La), Tau
PADRE PADRONE, P. and V. Taviani [FATHER, MASTER]

1977
BLACK STALLION (The), Ballard
CIAO MASCHIO, Ferreri [BYE BYE MONKEY]
COMMEDIE DI EDUARDO (Le), De Filippo
DOPPIO DELITTO, Steno
GATTO (Il), Comencini
IN NOME DEL PAPA RE, Magni
MADAME BOVARY, D'Anza
YETI, Kramer

1978
ALBERO DEGLI ZOCCOLI (L'), Olmi [THE TREE OF WOODEN CLOGS]
AMO NON AMO, Balducci [TOGETHER]
GIACCA VERDE (La), Giraldi
INGORGO (L'), Comencini
LUNA (La), B. Bertolucci
PRATO (Il), P. and V. Taviani
PROVA D'ORCHESTRA, Fellini [ORCHESTRA REHEARSAL]
TURI E I PALADINI, D'Alessandro
UMANOIDE (L'), Lewis [THE HUMANOID]
VIZIETTO (Il), Molinaro [LA CAGE AUX FOLLES/BIRDS OF A FEATHER]

1979
ACTION, Brass
BAMBULÈ, Modugno
BUONE NOTIZIE, Petri
CHIEDO ASILO, Ferreri
CITTÀ DELLE DONNE (La), Fellini [THE CITY OF WOMEN]
FEDORA, Wilder
GIOCATTOLO (Il), Montaldo
IMPROVVISO, Bruck
JONAS, Tanner [JONAS – WHO WILL BE 25 IN THE YEAR 2000]
MALEDETTI VI AMERÒ, Giordana
MASOCH, Brogi-Taviani

MOLIÈRE, Mnouchkine
ORIENT EXPRESS, Gantillon-D'Anza
RATATAPLAN, Nichetti
REIETTO DELLE ISOLE (Un), Moser
SI SALVI CHI VUOLE, Faenza
STARK SISTEM, Balducci
STORIE ALLO SPECCHIO, Albano-Ricci-Faccini
UN SACCO BELLO, Verdone
UOMINI E NO, Orsini
VIAGGIATORI DELLA SERA (I), Tognazzi
VITA DI GIUSEPPE VERDI (La), Castellani

1980
ANGELO E LA SIRENA (L'), Quilici
BIANCO, ROSSO E VERDONE, Verdone
BOSCO D'AMORE, Bevilacqua
CAMMINA, CAMMINA, Olmi
CANTO D'AMORE, Tattoli
MINESTRONE (Il), Citti
MISTERO DI OBERWALD (Il), Antonioni [THE OBERWALD MYSTERY]
PASSIONE D'AMORE, Scola
PELLE (La), Cavani

1981
BLACK STALLION RETURNS (The), Dalva
CADUTA DEGLI ANGELI RIBELLI (La), Giordana
CASA CECILIA, De Sisti
MARCHESE DEL GRILLO (Il), Monicelli
MONDO NUOVO (Il), Scola
NOTTE DI SAN LORENZO (La), P. and V. Taviani [THE NIGHT OF SAN LORENZO]
NUDO DI DONNA, Manfredi
PER FAVORE OCCUPATI DI AMELIA, Mogherini
SOGNI D'ORO, Moretti
STORIA D'AMORE E D'AMICIZIA, Rossi
STORIE DI ORDINARIA FOLLIA, Ferreri [TALES OF ORDINARY MADNESS]
TEMPEST, Mazursky
TRAGEDIA DI UN UOMO RIDICOLO (La), B. Bertolucci [THE TRAGEDY OF A RIDICULOUS MAN]

1982
ARRIVANO I MIEI, Salerno
BONNIE E CLYDE ALL'ITALIANA, Steno
CAMERA DELLE SIGNORE (La), Yannick
C'ERA UNA VOLTA IN AMERICA, Leone [ONCE UPON A TIME IN AMERICA]
CONTE TACCHIA (Il), Corbucci
COPKILLER, Faenza [ORDER OF DEATH]
CORSARO (Il), Giraldi
DOMANI SI BALLA, Nichetti
E LA NAVE VA, Fellini [AND THE SHIP SAILS ON]
GROG, Laudadio
IDENTIFICAZIONE DI UNA DONNA, Antonioni [IDENTIFICATION OF A WOMAN]
IN VIAGGIO CON PAPÀ, Sordi
IO SO CHE TU SAI CHE IO SO, Sordi
OCCHI, LA BOCCA (Gli), Bellocchio [THOSE EYES, THAT MOUTH]
PIANETA AZZURRO (Il), Piavoli
REGINA, Prate
SPECCHIO DEL DESIDERIO (Lo), Beineix
STATE BUONI SE POTETE, Magni
STORIA DI PIERA, Ferreri
TRAVIATA (La), Zeffirelli

1983
AMORE TOSSICO, Caligari
BALLANDO BALLANDO, Scola [LE BAL]
CANI DI GERUSALEMME, Carpi
CHIAVE (La), Brass [THE KEY]
CUORE, Comencini
DESIDERIO, Tatò
DON CHISCIOTTE, Scaparro
FLIRT, Russo

KAOS, P. and V. Taviani [CHAOS]
LADYHAWKE, Donner
LEGATI DA TENERA AMICIZIA, Giannetti
LO CHIAMAVANO DON CAMILLO, Hill
PIANOFORTE, F. Comencini
SCHERZO DEL DESTINO . . ., Wertmüller [THE JOKE OF FATE]
SOGNO DI UNA NOTTE DI MEZZA ESTATE, Salvatore
SOTTO . . . SOTTO . . . STRAPAZZATO DA ANOMALA PASSIONE, Wertmüller [A JEALOUS MAN/SOFTLY . . . SOFTLY]
SPAGHETTI HOUSE, Angeli
TASSINARO (Il), Sordi
TESORO PERDUTO, Zarindast

1984
BACIAMI STREGA, Tessari
DAGOBERT, Risi
DUE VITE DI MATTIA PASCAL (Le), Monicelli
ERA UNA NOTTE BUIA E TEMPESTOSA . . ., Benvenuti
FATTO SU MISURA, Laudadio
FIGLIO MIO INFINITAMENTE CARO, Orsini
FUTURO È DONNA (Il), Ferreri [THE FUTURE IS WOMAN]
HERBE ROUGE (L'), Kast
KING DAVID, Beresford
LIBERTÉ, EGALITÉ, CHOUCROUTE, Yanne
MACCHERONI, Scola [MACARONI]
MISTERO DEL MORCA (Il), Mattolini
NOI TRE, Pupi Avati
NON CI RESTA CHE PIANGERE, Benigni-Troisi
PIZZA CONNECTION, Damiani [THE SICILIAN CONNECTION]
RAGAZZO DI CAMPAGNA (Il), Castellano-Pipolo
SAVING GRACE, Young
SCUGNIZZO A NEW YORK (Uno), Laurenti
SEGRETI SEGRETI, G. Bertolucci [SECRETS, SECRETS]
SOGNI E BISOGNI, Citti
VOGLIA DI VOLARE, Murgia

1985
BALLATA DI EVA (La), Longo
BONNE (La), Samperi
CAGE AUX FOLLES III, Lautner [THE WEDDING]
CI VORREBBE UN AMICO, Montesano
COMPLICATO INTRIGO DI DONNE, VICOLI E DELITTI (Un), Wertmüller [CAMORRA: THE NAPLES CONNECTION]
DONNA DEL TRAGHETTO (La), Fago
EMBASSY, Lewis
FIFTH MISSILE (The), Peerce
GINGER E FRED, Fellini [GINGER AND FRED]
IO SONO UN FENOMENO PARANORMALE, Corbucci
JOAN LUI, Celentano
MAI CON LE DONNE, Fago
MALEDETTO TRENO, Laurenti
MESSA È FINITA (La), Moretti
MIRANDA, Brass
MOMO, Schaaf
MOSTRO DI FIRENZE (Il), Ferrario
NAME OF THE ROSE (The), Annaud
ONORA IL PADRE, Ferrari
ORFEO, Goretta [ORPHEUS]
OTELLO, Zeffirelli [OTHELLO]
POMPIERI (I), Neri Parenti
SE UN GIORNO BUSSERAI ALLA MIA PORTA, Perilli
SEPARATI IN CASA, Pazzaglia
SOTTO IL VESTITO NIENTE, Vanzina [NOTHING UNDERNEATH]
SPINA NEL CUORE (Una), Lattuada
TERNO SECCO, Giannini
TEX E IL SIGNORE DEGLI ABISSI, Tessari
TROPPO FORTE, Verdone

1986
BURBERO (Il), Castellano e Pipolo
DAY BEFORE (The), Montaldo
FAMIGLIA (La), Scola [THE FAMILY]
GIORNI DELL'IRA (I), Ferrara
GOOD MORNING BABILONIA, P. and V. Taviani [GOOD MORNING BABYLON]
GRANDI MAGAZZINI (I), Castellano and Pipolo

HELENA, Soldi
HOMME AMOUREUX (Un), Kurys [A MAN IN LOVE]
I LOVE N.Y., Bozzacchi
INTERVISTA (L'), Fellini
MAN OF FIRE, Chouraquie
MONACA DI MONZA (La), Odorisio
MOSCA ADDIO, Bolognini
SUPERFANTOZZI, Parenti
ULTIMO IMPERATORE (L'), B. Bertolucci [THE LAST EMPEROR]
UOMINI DURI, Ponzi
VIA MONTENAPOLEONE, C. Vanzina

1987
ACQUARIO, Rosati
AFFITTASI, Neri Parenti
ARRIVEDERCI E GRAZIE, Capitani
BARONE MUNCHAUSEN, Gilliam [THE ADVENTURES OF BARON MUNCHAUSEN]
BOHÈME (La), Comencini
DA GRANDE, Amurri
DONNA SPEZZATA (La), Leto
E NON SE NE VOGLIONO ANDARE, Capitani
GAME OVER, Orfini
INVESTIGATORI PRIVATI, Di Tillo
IO E MIA SORELLA, Verdone
PANINO ASSASSINO, Soldi
PIAZZA NAVONA, various directors
PICARI (I), Monicelli
PRICELESS BEAUTY, Finch
RENEGADE, E. B. Clucher
ROSSA VIA PARADISO, Odorisio
RUSSICUM, Squitieri
SILENT NIGHT, Tauber
SNACK BAR BUDAPEST, Brass
STORIA DI UNA DONNA, Vanzina
STRADIVARI, Battiato
TEATRO N, Russo
TOPO GALILEO, Laudadio
TURNO DI NOTTE, Argento
VISIONE DEL SABBA (La), Bellocchio
ZOO, Comencini

INDEX

PICTURE SOURCES

Pino Abbrescia 30, 31, 32–33
Archivio Cinecittà 8, 9, 10–11, 15, 16, 17b, 22, 23, 25, 29ac, 102–103
Archivio Mondadori 66b, 121a
Archivio PEA 76–77
Tiziana Callari 2, 6
Mimmo Cattarinich 81a
Osvaldo Civirani 72, 73
Farabola Foto 14, 26–27
Grazia Neri 24
Emilio Lari, 16, 17a 18–19, 20, 21, 22, 158–159, 159, 161b
Franco Pinna, 12, 13, 64, 66a, 68–69, 70, 71, 75, 78–79, 80, 81b, 82–83, 84, 86–87, 88, 89, 90–91, 92, 93, 96, 97, 98–99, 99, 100, 103b, 104, 106–107, 109, 110–111, 114, 116–117, 120–121b, 122, 123, 126b, 130–131
Pierluigi Praturlon 25as, 29b, 34, 35, 36, 37, 38, 39, 40, 41, 42, 43, 44, 47, 65, 73as, 112, 118, 126a, 128, 129, 133, 142, 156, 157, 160, 161a
Paul Ronald 48, 49, 51, 52–53, 55, 56, 57, 58, 59, 62–63, 63, 163
Studio Fotografico Roberto Russo 148–149, 149, 150, 151, 152–153, 153, 154, 155
Tazio Secchiaroli 50, 61
Gabriele Stocchi, 137, 138, 139, 140, 141, 143, 144, 144–145, 145, 147

The abbreviations a, b, c, d, s, refer to the position of the illustration on the page (above, below, center, right, left).